A PLUME BOOK

HOW TO RUIN EVERYTHING

JARED LEIBOWITZ

GEORGE WATSKY is a writer and musician originally from San Francisco. After getting his start in spoken-word poetry, Watsky became better known as a rapper and touring musician. As a teenager, George appeared on the final season of *Russell Simmons Presents Def Poetry* on HBO and subsequently performed at hundreds of universities across the country, while himself enrolled at Emerson College. Using the money from his college shows to fund his early music videos, George's fast rapping went viral in 2011. Watsky has released a number of mixtapes and full albums, his most recent, 2013's *Cardboard Castles* and 2014's *All You Can Do,* which peaked, respectively, at #7 and #6 on the iTunes charts. A versatile writer, his solo theater piece, *So Many Levels,* was presented in Boston, San Francisco, Vermont, and at the Hip Hop Theater Festival Critical Breaks series in New York City.

D1019963

Praise for *How to Ruin Everything*

"Watsky is a skillful lyricist who has successfully transferred his wit, humor, and humility into a smartly written collection of essays. *How to Ruin Everything* shows off his versatility as a writer and proves that the nerdy guys can also be part of the cool crowd."   —Russell Simmons

"George Watsky is a lyrical mastermind. Unflinchingly honest, sincere, and gut-wrenchingly funny, *How to Ruin Everything* is one of the best books I've read this year. Watsky effortlessly translates his razor-sharp wit from the stage to the page. This will be the first of many amazing books in the life of a tireless artist."   —Hasan Minhaj, *The Daily Show* correspondent

"In *How To Ruin Everything*, George Watsky sets off around the world to find out why nothing ever explodes the way it should—not fireworks, spicy foods, hip hop, sex with middle-aged women, or minor criminal activities. Along the way he captures how it feels to be young, in beautiful writing that is compulsively readable, gut-clutchingly funny, and deeply humane. Don't miss it."

—Jeff Chang, author *Can't Stop Won't Stop*, *Who We Be*, and
We Gon' Be Alright

"At their best, these essays are incisive and soulful, suffused with scorching wit, careful observation, and probing self-awareness. And at their worst, they're still funnier than anything you're likely to hear at your city's most entertaining bar, even if you drink there every night for a month. Which you might have to, in order to process the fact that a guy who looks like he's twelve just wrote the best debut essay collection of the year."

—Adam Mansbach, #1 *New York Times* bestselling
author of *Go the F**k to Sleep*

"He reminds me of myself, only a better writer than I can."

—Rhys Darby, *Flight of the Conchords*

"When George Watsky raps, the quantity and quality of his words and concepts often flow so quickly that you can only hope to let them wash over your consciousness and bathe in their essence, because it's impossible to stop time and live appreciatively in each individual moment. Thankfully, though, in this collection of his writings, you can do just that, because that's how reading works. You can examine every drop of Watsky's kindness, thoughtfulness, self-awareness, curiosity, and adventurousness, seeing how he is continually and/or continuously growing as an artist and a human, and you will, too."

—Myq Kaplan, comic featured on *Conan, Last Comic Standing,* and *The Late Show with David Letterman*

"*How to Ruin Everything* is laugh-out-loud funny, painfully honest, and subversively sincere. Watsky speaks boundlessly and insightfully about the life of a creative person. It is instantly relatable, clever, sharp, and observant."

—Jonny Sun, creator of the popular @jonnysun Twitter comedy account and MIT doctoral candidate

"George Watsky does again what he does best: attaches disarming, unparalleled wit to the mundane, making meditation of the routine and human. Everything you've come to expect from Watsky the rapper and George the poet is housed in this brilliant and unmatched collection of essays. His unique approach to rhythm is buoyed by his precision of idea and economy of language. . . . An instant classic."

—Chinaka Hodge, author of *Dated Emcees*

How to Ruin Everything

Essays

GEORGE WATSKY

A PLUME BOOK

PLUME
An imprint of Penguin Random House LLC
375 Hudson Street
New York, New York 10014

 REGISTERED TRADEMARK—MARCA REGISTRADA

Library of Congress Cataloging-in-Publication Data
Names: Watsky, 1986– author.
Title: How to ruin everything : essays / George Watsky.
Description: New York, New York : Plume, 2016.
Identifiers: LCCN 2015048700 (print) | LCCN 2015050851 (ebook) | ISBN
    9780147515995 (paperback) | ISBN 9780698191242 (eBook)
Subjects: LCSH: Watsky, 1986—Humor. | Poets, American—Biography. | Rap
    musicians—United States—Biography. | BISAC: HUMOR / Form / Essays. |
    BIOGRAPHY & AUTOBIOGRAPHY / Personal Memoirs. | HUMOR / General.
Classification: LCC PS3623.A86964 A6 2016 (print) | LCC PS3623.A86964 (ebook)
    | DDC 814/.6—dc23
LC record available at http://lccn.loc.gov/2015048700

Printed in the United States of America
10 9 8 7 6 5 4 3 2

For Mom
and all librarians

Contents

How to Ruin
Everything

Introduction

There is no book so bad . . . that it does not have something good in it.

—Miguel de Cervantes Saavedra, *Don Quixote*

I started writing these pieces as a form of self-reflection follow-ing a series of dumb and personally destructive decisions. *How come if people keep telling me I'm so smart, I keep doing such stupid things?* I pondered.

The stories in this book touch on many delightful strategies for self-sabotage, all pulled from the kaleidoscope of my personal-ity: hubris, egotism, carelessness, laziness, stubbornness, lust, fear, self-hatred, neurosis, and more. If some positive qualities seep into your impression of me along the way, remember that *I* wrote this and personal essaying is propaganda of the highest order, so any-thing that makes me look cool is also an example of my narcissism.

I truly hope you get something good out of *How to Ruin Every-thing.* If you come away with a bit of entertainment or a cautionary lesson or even just tear out some pages, fold them up, and use them

1

to balance a wobbly table, I won't have wasted all this paper for nothing. And perhaps, if you truly aspire to ruin everything, it's best you stop reading right now. For I came to a troubling conclusion as I neared this book's completion: The only good way to ruin everything is by accident—if you make an effort to do it you've *tried*, and sadly, trying is its own success. Unfortunately, by the time I had this realization, Penguin was already marketing the book and it was too late to change the name. I had a good cry until it occurred to me that at least I'd succeeded in failing to deliver on the promise of the title. And that may not be "everything," but hey, nobody's perfect.

GEORGE

Tusk

The Los Angeles neighborhood of Mid-City is notable mostly for being between other places. A district surrounded by 'woods (Holly and Ingle) to the north and south, downtown and Santa Monica to the east and west, Mid-City's in the dead center of town—the Oklahoma of LA—and my college friends and I lived there for a year following graduation, a block and a half from a recent string of grisly point-blank shotgun murders and the densest concentration of tire shops in the known universe. If I ever worked for the board of tourism, I'd propose: "Mid-City: Weird spot to raise a kid, great place to catch a flat!" But there must have been children because, although I never saw them, there was apparently enough demand to support a Kinder Kids daycare center on our corner, directly across the street from City Spa, our seedy neighborhood bathhouse. Kinder Kids' towering blue yard walls were ringed with dense coils of barbed wire—not garden-variety tear-your-jeans barbed wire, but the industrial-strength, leg-amputation type: huge, jagged steel teeth I imagined were blow-torched from the hulls of discarded navy warships. It kept the predators from crawling in and it kept the kids from crawling out.

We'd relocated from Boston to our one-story Spanish, clay-roofed house together. It's a tired script: four college kids coming to take Hollywood by storm. We were off to a slow start, and Mid-City didn't feel any closer to The Industry than Boston. We could see Hollywood faintly from our house, far beyond Kinder Kids, ringed with high fences and iron spines of its own, but we spent our days on the outside in limbo. After an appearance on a late-night HBO poetry showcase a few years earlier, my ambitions as a rapper and beloved public figure had stalled. Occasionally I'd fly to the real Oklahoma for a spoken-word gig at a college coffee-house, but mostly we congealed on the couch, watching hours of *Deadliest Catch*, looking for work, waiting for our phones to ring, generally really, really bored. *Between-things.*

One August night I sat at our backyard fire pit drinking and talking summer plans with my obliviously handsome aspiring-filmmaker roommate Jackson. In a few weeks he was heading to Denver for his great-aunt June's hundredth birthday party. I hadn't met her yet, but Aunt June's legend cast an imposing shadow. She was a woman, Jackson told me, with a big imagination, but it was a blood-splattered, *Grimms' Fairy Tales*–type fantasy; she loved anything exotic, petrified, or taxidermied. Aunt June was a self-described "rock hound"—someone who visits geological trade shows the way Dead Heads follow tour stops. She and her son, a conservative in his midseventies, spent their free time bartering gemstones and fossilized trilobites at warehouses that alternated weekends between rodeos and monster truck rallies. When Aunt June meets you, if she likes you, she'll slide you a small piece of quartz, which she expects you to carry around as a personal talisman. Should you cross paths with her in the future and she produces her own piece of quartz, saying "match me!" you're expected to whip out your rock. If you can't "match" June, you owe her a nickel. If you can, she owes you. Aunt June was all about results—match her, and she'll respect you forever. Fail her, and you won't get a second chance.

June also had a very specific obsession: narwhals. This arctic whale, a cousin of the beluga, is fabled for its single huge tusk, actually an overgrown canine tooth blasted through its lip. When I finally met Aunt June I saw that her house was decorated floor to ceiling in narwhal images: colorful pop-up construction paper narwhals, glass narwhal figurines, and, on the refrigerator, a photograph of her lording over a bloody narwhal carcass, its horn hacksawed from its skull. The picture was taken a few years earlier during a cruise to the Canadian Arctic with her son. After the animal had been cleaned, she legally purchased its tusk from the Inuit village through a loophole in endangered species law, allowing native Canadians to continue traditional hunts in support of their local economy. Aunt June loved that tusk. Of all her trinkets, tchotchkes, and pieces of crap, it was her favorite.

Unfortunately for Aunt June, narwhal tusks are classified as ivory, and it's illegal to traffic ivory across the US border. The law was established to protect against African elephant poaching, but narwhals were caught in the same legal dragnet. So an irritated

Aunt June was forced to abandon her tusk in Vancouver, where for years it gathered dust in her neighbor's daughter's closet despite her repeated pleas that her family make a reconnaissance mission on her behalf. Up to this point, no one had obliged.

As Jackson explained these circumstances, it occurred to us that this was a story we had a chance to write ourselves into. The drive from Los Angeles to Vancouver to Denver, then back to LA is an equilateral triangle—a thousand miles on each side, we estimated. Aunt June's birthday was in thirteen days. We had a car. We had more than enough time. And we had nothing better to do.

I'd been a vegetarian on *Bambi*–and–*Charlotte's Web* grounds for a decade, so I was initially conflicted. We were, after all, talking about trafficking a hacked-off hunk of a rare marine mammal that had been hunted, gutted, photographed for a Colorado scrapbook, and sold for parts. And there was the small inconvenience of the law. But still. After a person turns twenty-one, most milestone birthdays are ominous reminders of our mortality: thirty, forty, fifty, sixty—potentially depressing moments in a person's life. But One Hundred is a double middle-finger salute to the reaper. If Aunt June was really about to make it across the longest yard, who were we to deny her wishes? She grew up in the days when lamps ran on whale blubber, guitars were strung with catgut, and pig brains were a delicacy. Imposing my pampered millennial morality on the situation would be an insult to her entire generation.

The more Jackson and I talked, the closer I inched to the bottom of my Steel Reserve bottle, the more obvious it all became. I

don't think anyone ever plans to become an international ivory
smuggler. It just happens one day.

August 12

Like many restless people, I love driving. Driving gives me a destination and a purpose—watching new landscapes peel back one
after another over the horizon is a great way to simulate progress.
My junior year of high school, when I was going through a particularly insomniac stretch of anxiety, I'd lie on my back staring up at
the long crack in my ceiling plaster carved by the 1989 Loma Prieta
earthquake. When I couldn't stare anymore I'd call up a friend and
take a midnight trip in my mom's silver Volvo station wagon—the
150-mile round trip to Santa Cruz, the 300 miles to Lake Tahoe and
back—at one point 1,300 miles to Portland—only to turn around
and come home without telling my parents I'd ever left.

But these days, I drove a practical blue Subaru hatchback, a
car that has for some reason become associated with lesbianism. I
take this to mean lesbians love unflashy, reliable vehicles that get
you from point A to point B, and if the Subaru hatchback isn't an
argument to make for the stability of same-gender families, I don't
know what is. My Outback might not have been the most glamor-
ous car for the job, but next to Jackson's mint-green '94 Camry
and its busted AC, it was the obvious choice, and I drafted it into
service.

Our friend Zach hitched a ride with us up to San Francisco, and Jackson and I plotted as we plunged out of the mountains near Fort Tejon into the strawberry fields of the Central Valley. By the time we rolled up our windows to block the stink at the Harris Cattle Ranch, we fully realized how poorly we'd prepared for the opera-tion. I'd thrown a couple of days' worth of clothes into a little purple backpack I reserved for trips out of town and we'd made contact with Lydia, the keeper of the tusk, in Vancouver. But we hadn't thought much about the *crime* part of the crime. Namely, how we'd hide four feet of felonious ivory in my unlocked trunk from border agents whose job it was to find it. We turned off Highway 5 at Modesto and detoured toward Yosemite, weighing our options.

We could stash the tusk in the wall paneling of the car. We could wrap it in a blanket and strap it onto the ski rack. We could sew it into the uphol-stery of a piece of furniture or lash it under the chassis. In any creative endeavor you discard a bunch of terrible ideas before you land on a good one. We had a lot of bad ideas. Ultimately, we agreed the best tactic was the simplest: Cover it up in the back of the car, hide it in plain sight, hope not to get searched, and play dumb if busted. We figured it was a plan to match our vehicle—unspectacular and solid. It would work, as long as we didn't run into any surprises.

We ran into our first surprise forty minutes down Highway 132. I don't know why, but tires like to go flat just after 5:00 P.M., when mechanics close up shop. By the time we noticed we were losing air, we'd driven too far down the winding, single-lane road to turn around, and sure enough, once we wobbled into the dusty old mining town of Coulterville, its red tin–roofed general store and service station was shuttered for the day. We pulled over and yanked a long nail from our deflated front right tire. We were beyond cell reception, miles from the nearest AAA affiliate, and only a few hours into our trip, Mid-City's thick forest of tire shops laughing at us from afar.

Eventually we figured out how to use the car jack in the trunk and rolled into Tuolumne Meadows, leaning left on our mini donut tire, Half Dome's and El Capitan's huge granite faces peeking diagonally over the dashboard. We stopped for dinner at the village where an old San Francisco friend of mine named Laura was working as a park ranger. Laura and I had escaped our high school physical ed requirements by taking salsa lessons together, and now she was Yosemite's chief archivist—the gatekeeper for any academics who wanted to conduct research in the park. Of anyone on the planet with a good reason to be pissed off about ivory smuggling, I'd think it would be a forest ranger. But my old gym-evading accomplice Laura understood moral compromise—that sometimes conservation and love can't coexist neatly. So she gave our mission her blessing, and we left the park on the donut tire that night. No service stations would be open until morning, and we limped the last three hours on the freeway to San Francisco, hugging the right lane.

August 13

By random universal symmetry, our route took us straight to my dad's birthday party in the Bay Area. After dropping Zach off in the Mission and changing our tire, we headed to Inverness, just outside of Point Reyes on the rural coast of West Marin. My parents still live in the same San Francisco home I grew up in, but they'd been spending more and more time at the Inverness house that's been in my mom's family since the fifties. It was rented to strangers for most of my life, but with the kids gone, my folks had moved back in part-time. Old Bolinas beat poets, my dad's best friend, Saul, and the rest of his psychologist buddies shuffled around eating barbeque on the rebuilt wooden deck where my parents had said their vows thirty years earlier—maybe twenty people, but by my dad's standards a wild rager. I can't remember why Dad had a big sixty-eighth birthday celebration when he let seventy slip by quietly, but he's never been a slave to round numbers.

I know they're meaningless—round numbers—but I like them anyway. Humans assign significance to multiples of ten only because we ended up with ten fingers, and if hands had evolved with six fingers we'd be going nuts at twelfth, twenty-fourth, thirty-sixth, and forty-eighth birthdays. But we didn't and since I was a kid I'd always wanted to be a part of a triple-digit celebration— no small factor in my eagerness to glom onto Aunt June's glory. I hadn't been close with my father's mother, my last living grandparent, and when she died at ninety-nine years and eleven months, I grieved the round number's demise as much as Grandma's. My dad was simply relieved to say good-bye to a domineering and controlling mother who he didn't think deserved the centennial honor. I saw in Grandma Syde shades of the toughness Jackson described in Aunt June, but there was a fundamental difference in style—if June wanted something, no matter how unreasonable, she'd look you in the eye and ask. Syde preferred subtle manipulation, and the kind and cautious man my dad grew into was shaped by what he absorbed from his mom, but even more so by what he vowed never to become.

All I brought my father for his birthday were more reasons to worry about me. He was conflicted about our heist. On the one hand, he's a law-abiding Jew(ish) man who's been concerned about every poor choice I've ever made, and even some of the good ones. On the other hand, my dad understands tusks. A borderline rock hound who gave me a stuffed dead iguana for my tenth birthday, he has a decades-tall pile of old *National Geographic* magazines in the corner of his study. Dad interned at the American Museum of Natural History as a teenager around 1960, and when he took me to tour his old haunt on a family trip to Manhattan he nostalgically pointed out every butterfly display in the twisting hallways he could still navigate easily, trying to excite me about evolution and how life can be organized and understood.

He'd worked at the museum under a dedicated but unashamedly colonialist ornithologist named J. P. Chapin. Author of 1932's *Birds of the Belgian Congo*, Chapin was proud to have proved the existence of the long-rumored Congo peacock but ambivalent about the fact that he'd shot and killed the only known member of a rare variety of scarlet African finch, simultaneously discovering the species and snuffing it out with the same bullet. Chapin was the seventeenth president of the famed Explorers Club, the most prestigious of that era's popular white-guys-discovering-things-that-are-already-there societies.

And in 1951, when members excavated a fully intact wooly mammoth in the Siberian icepack, its flesh preserved like a ten-thousand-year-old brisket in the freezer, their first instinct wasn't to arrange a public viewing but to instead organize an exclusive mammoth banquet for themselves. Because for these men of science, the most pressing intellectual question raised by this huge discovery was *I wonder what the fuck it tastes like.* Hearing this, at ten years old, it made perfect sense to me.

August 14—August 15

After leaving San Francisco we drove through Northern California's Trinity Alps, where my aunt and uncle have a small cabin near Hyampom. Jackson and I spent a day skipping rocks and pointing out eagles and dragonflies before heading farther north. Our next stop was Seattle, where Jackson's brother worked as a water taxi captain, getting up at 4:00 A.M. to shuttle mainlanders to their jobs on small coastal islands. The night before driving into Canada, Jackson and I spent our last pre-smuggler hours huddled in blankets in the dark living room, imagining worst-case scenarios.

"He was selling weed in Mexico and they pinned two murders on him," Jackson recalled from *Locked Up Abroad*, his favorite reality show about law-breaking travelers who find themselves . . . *locked up abroad.* In Jackson's version of each story, the perp wound up trapped forever in byzantine courts, eating maggot-riddled biscuits, growing old cut off from his family, and scratching at the stone walls of a dungeon shared with a hulking, sexually insatiable cellmate named Tiny.

We decided by coin flip that Jackson would drive us into Canada and I would drive us out. But as we passed along the green stretch of mountain-lined road that connects Seattle with the border, finally faced with some actual risk, the daring adventure we'd penned ourselves into as heroes started fading. *There's no shame in quitting,* we softly suggested. Only there was—dishonorable, devastating shame. And despite the advancing web of gloom, we crawled closer and closer to Canada, eventually settling into the line of cars at Customs.

When we reached the border kiosk, Jackson did the talking.

"Passports, please. What's the purpose of your visit to Canada?"

"Visiting a family friend."

Jackson handed over our passports.

"What are you going to be doing with your friend?"

"We're going," Jackson replied, sticking to our planned alibi, "on a hike."

"A hike? Where are you hiking?"

We hadn't talked through the details of our cover story any further than "a hike." Jackson swallowed.

"I don't know."

The agent looked up from leafing through our passports.

"Do you have any drugs, weapons, or alcohol on you?"

"No," Jackson responded, unconvincingly.

"Drive to the right. Park and wait in the Customs office."

We watched through the office window as the canine unit sniffed my doors and an agent riffled through the car, removing and replacing each item.

"They're not gonna find anything," Jackson leaned over on the bench and whispered to me, "right?"

"SSSSHHHHH!!!" the desk officer hissed.

I shrugged at Jackson. We'd made an effort to toss any contraband before the border. After stalemating in an argument over whether dogs can smell psychedelics we'd even ditched my last foil-covered shroom chocolate at his brother's place in Seattle, so we had every reason to believe we were clean. And indeed, the agent outside gave up and walked toward our holding room.

"Which one of you's George?" he asked, striding through the door. I raised my hand and trudged somberly up to the desk.

"So you're a musician, huh?"

"Sort of."

"Going on tour soon?"

The officer handed me my monthly planner sternly, then flashed a smile.

"Have fun!"

Although we sighed as he stamped our passports and issued us the pink immigration form that officially welcomed us to Canada, the border search still felt like a grim omen—one that we speculated placed us on some international Shady Characters watch list—a list guaranteeing our search on the way out of the country. After we pulled out of the border checkpoint we headed straight to Vancouver, careful not to do anything else that could arouse suspicion. Once our phones switched into global roaming we called Lydia to let her know we were on our way, taking in the eerie foreign landscape of Tim Hortons, kilometer markers, and sleepy side streets as we approached her house.

"If you think this is quiet, you should have been here in June when the Canucks lost the Cup finals," Lydia said when we arrived. "You could hear the hearts breaking."

Lydia's Vancouver apartment was spotless and minimally decorated. I waited impatiently through her and Jackson's gossip about vague mutual friends shared through Aunt June back in Denver, until she led us to her bedroom. The four-foot tusk already lay cradled in a fold of her comforter. It was a stunning piece of biological engineering—a mathematically perfect ridge spiraled in wide and lazy arcs around the base and then in tighter and tighter rings at the tip. The tusk was sturdy, lethal, and beautiful all at once, both ghostly and concrete. I could see why Aunt June was obsessed. And even though Lydia knew we were coming to pick up the tusk and seemed happy to help the cause, she wavered when the moment finally came to hand it over. As Jackson moved to take the black PVC pipe encasing it, Lydia's forehead creased and a flicker of Gollum-like envy burned in her eyes. But after a moment her fingers loosened, and the tusk was ours.

In the kitchen Lydia prepared our bounty for transit, shaking a few loose ivory flakes from the bottom of the pipe into her palm—fragments from the tusk's jagged base, where the horn once met the narwhal's skull—and moved toward her trash can. It occurred to me that narwhal tusk, even in small shavings, probably held some kind of spirit-warding/aphrodisiac/hallucinogenic/otherwise-magical power.

"Wait—I'll keep them as a souvenir."

She placed the flakes in a Ziploc bag and handed it to me, and we walked outside to hide the pipe in my trunk. The three of us discussed our getaway plans as I scattered dirty laundry over the tusk. Jackson and I figured it might be best to wait until the middle of the night and cross under the cloak of darkness, which meant we had time to kill.

"Why don't you *really* come hike the Grind with me?" Lydia asked.

There's a small ski resort called Grouse Mountain on the outskirts of Vancouver. In the summer you can climb the slope, a vertical-mile route seasonally rebranded "the Grind" to appeal to the masochistic fitness nuts who dominate the city. Lydia happened to be training that afternoon for an upcoming triathlon, as I was stunned to learn normal Canadians sometimes do. We already knew Lydia was planning a hike—it had formed the basis of our shitty alibi on the way across the border—but the best way to improve a shitty alibi, we reasoned, was to live it.

The three of us, joined by two of Lydia's Lululemon-encased exercise buddies, jogged from the parking lot to the base of the mountain just as an attendant was swinging the wrought-iron door shut.

"No more hikers. The mountain is closing!" the guard yelled.

Lydia wedged into the gate with her shoulder, making enough daylight for the rest of us to slip in behind her. A loud metallic clang sealed us in and we were greeted by a series of alarming notices: HIKERS USING THESE TRAILS ASSUME ALL LIABILITY OF PERSONAL INJURY OR DEATH RESULTING FROM ANY CAUSE WHATSOEVER, INCLUDING BUT NOT LIMITED TO AVALANCHES, CLIFFS, ROCKFALLS, GULLIES, RAVINES, WATERFALLS, RAPIDLY CHANGING WEATHER CONDITIONS, ENCOUNTERS WITH DOMESTIC OR WILD ANIMALS ... A separate sign warning of recent black bear sightings hung on a nearby fence. *What's the difference between a gully and a ravine?* I wondered. *That's an incredibly specific differentiation.* I assume the gully deaths list had filled up and they'd had to start a new one for people who fell into ravines. The guard called lazily after us one more time—she had mentally clocked out of her shift, her only remaining responsibility to make us aware there'd be no one to retrieve our corpses from the mountainside.

"Meet you guys at the top."

Lydia and her friends darted off like roadrunners and were out of sight in seconds.

The Grind is so steep that wooden steps—really more of a ladder—have been hammered into the hill. Jackson and I struggled up to the quarter-progress marker, meditating on the irony that we were going to die on a Canadian mountain before we even got the chance to burglarize the country. I gasped as our couch potato bodies crumbled one increasingly painful step at a time, all our anxieties pooling together and foaming over. Still only halfway up the mountain, Jackson looked at me, red-faced and wild-eyed.

"I think we're gonna go to jail."

When we did finally make it to the top, we learned the gondola back down to the bottom was broken. We weren't too bothered. As our pulses settled we stared out over Vancouver's beautiful skyline panorama, tinged pink in the sunset, grateful not to be rotting in a ravine. And after mechanics finally fixed the bug, we rode down the dusky mountain feeling bulletproof.

We said good-bye to Lydia and waited until 1:00 A.M. to approach the border, figuring that's when exhausted Customs agents would be least likely to pause their Bejeweled game to cavity-search us. We drove in silence. Jackson's phone rang, his dad, awake at 4:00 A.M. in Western Massachusetts, insisting it wasn't too late to turn back. But our minds were made up, Jackson explained, then hung up and called his girlfriend.

"You'll either hear from us in twenty minutes," he warned her, "or things are bad." Then he asked the real question that had been gnawing at him.

"If I go to jail for five years, will you break up with me?"

We stared straight ahead, the kiosk growing bigger and bigger in front of us. This time there wasn't a line of cars to wait in. This time we were ready with our alibi, chock-full of real-life hiking details. I eased the brakes as we approached.

"Passports, please."

I handed them over as authoritatively as I could.

"Reason for visiting Canada?"

"We came to hike the Grind."

The border agent scanned our documents and handed our passports back.

"Have a nice night."

I waited at the kiosk for the follow-up questions. But the agent just waved us along.

That was it?

We drove around a few final Canadian bends and the road shot us right back onto I-5, and into the United States. We craned our ears for the sound of sirens tailing us.

That was it.

We turned the radio to the first station we found, cranked the volume, and howled as we headed back toward Seattle. Jackson and I stopped at the first bar we passed, barely beating last call, and toasted ourselves, fears long forgotten—just two stone-cold smugglers, a thousand miles of open road, and four feet of contraband whale tooth.

August 16

There are two main routes from Vancouver to Denver. The southern path lops a corner off of Oregon, makes a detour through Utah, and sneaks along the bottom of Wyoming before dropping into Colorado. The northern route takes you across most of Montana before traversing Wyoming lengthwise, making stops in Casper and Cheyenne. For whatever reason, we chose to go north and enjoyed hundreds of miles of dense, sunny evergreen forests on our way to Billings, where we booked a cheap family-owned motel room for the night.

We pulled into Billings after midnight, but I missed the left turn for our hotel. The streets were barren, so I swung wide and

U-turned in the middle of the block, slicing across the double yellow lines.

"What are you doing?!" Jackson snapped.

"Come on, there's no one around."

I was annoyed, but he made a fair point. We had plenty of time to get to Denver if we stayed the course. Any unnecessary risks were stupid. So we made an agreement: No traffic violations. No speeding. Use cruise control whenever possible.

I eased carefully into the dirt lot and parked next to a row of semitrucks, a cloud of moths muting each hotel lamp.

August 17

I grew up under the impression that the real speed limit is ten miles an hour over whatever's posted on the sign. So I can't really blame Jackson for breaking his own rule—he'd set the cruise control at eighty-four in a seventy-five zone—but just a night before Aunt June's party, an hour from the Colorado border, we heard the *woop woop!* of sirens, the Rocky Mountains ahead of us flickering blue and red, police lights flashing in our rearview mirror.

It's just a speeding ticket, no cause for alarm, we assured each other as Jackson pulled over to the shoulder. A balding thirtysomething Wyoming highway patrolman sauntered up to Jackson's window.

"Do you know why I pulled you two over?" he leaned in to ask.

"I'm so sorry, Officer, I lost track of my speed," Jackson replied.

"License and registration. Where you gentlemen coming from?"

"Los Angeles. Then Vancouver. We're headed to Denver now."

The officer arched his bushy eyebrows.

"What were you boys doin' up in Vancouver?"

Jackson's eyes shifted. "Visiting family."

"Uh-huh." The patrolman craned his neck into the car.

"You boys wouldn't mind if I ask you some questions separately, would you?"

"Not at all," Jackson lied.

The officer sent Jackson to the back of his squad car and grilled him first, while I tried to guess the arc of the conversation from their hand gestures. After he'd interrogated Jackson to his satisfaction, the policeman walked back to me and the Subaru.

"I'm your friend," he assured me, "as long as you tell the truth."

Since Jackson and I hadn't had time to come up with a cover, I kept my story consistent with the facts: We drove from LA to San Francisco, where we celebrated my dad's birthday, visited Jackson's brother in Seattle, then our friend in Vancouver, and were now on our way to some old lady's birthday party in Denver.

"Do you have any drugs in the car?" the officer asked.

"No, sir."

"Okay, that's good. Reason I ask is because the route you're driving is a pretty popular drug triangle."

"It is?"

"It is. You wouldn't mind if I looked around the car a bit, would you?"

He squinted.

"I think I smelled something a little off in there."

I wasn't getting the sense he'd be receptive to a debate over probable cause, so I agreed to the search. After the officer guided Jackson and me to the side of the road and called for a backup car, he started rummaging through the front seats. I clung to the hope that the Wyoming Highway Patrol probably didn't have their eyes peeled for narwhal tusks, and he might not know what to make of it if he found it. He held his ear to the side panels and knocked carefully on the plastic, stopping when he made a discovery in the seatback pocket.

"And what's *this*?" the patrolman asked.

"That's a bottle of Advil," Jackson replied as the officer unscrewed the lid.

"I've only seen red Advils . . ." he muttered, replacing the container in my toiletry kit.

"They're Liqui-Gels."

His hunting got more and more frantic, working his way backward until he was finally in the trunk, digging through the loose clothes that hid our secret. As he started sifting through my little purple backpack, the corner of his lip turned up in a smirk.

"And what exactly is *this*?"

He raised a clear sack, packed with suspicious white flakes. Turns out from a distance, a Ziploc of tusk crumbs looks a lot like a meth baggie.

"It's shells"—I scrambled—"from the sea."

He squinted at the contents of the bag and returned it to my backpack, disappointed. And then, as he was right at the tusk, my teeth grinding, heart jackhammering, time slowing to a crawl, a grin bloomed fully across his face.

"And whose is *this?*" the officer asked smugly, lifting one last prize from the trunk.

Jackson and I exchanged an it-was-nice-knowing-you-buddy glance.

"Thought you boys said you didn't have any drugs."

The officer held up a little glass pipe. Not the giant tusk a few inches away. Not even the foil-covered mushroom chocolate that I'd retrieved in Seattle. But instead, an orphaned, baby one-hitter pipe in a pocket of my purple backpack, the bowl caked with the residue of a six-month-old smoke session—a piece that I barely remembered I owned—one that had somehow slipped undetected through a Canadian border search so thorough that the guard learned my upcoming social calendar—paraphernalia that could have derailed our mission before it had started but instead waited until our darkest hour to materialize.

"We don't like liars in Wyoming."

Before I knew it, I had my hands behind my back in the squad car, my cuffs taking piranha bites out of my wrists. Jackson, feeling guilty for speeding, begged the officer to be allowed to take my place. But instead, we pulled back onto Interstate 25 South, together but separate—Jackson behind the wheel of my Subaru, me in the back of the squad car, until I peeled off at exit 140 toward Douglas, and Jackson slipped over the horizon. The officer tsk-tsked me from behind the metal grating as he sped us to the station, oblivious to the career-making ivory bust disappearing behind him. Now Jackson was alone on the road, our prize still safe in the trunk, two hundred miles between him and Denver, fifteen hours until the party.

I was booked right away at the quiet Converse County police station. I handed the clerk my driver's license, still featuring the same smart-aleck pouty face I'd pulled at the San Francisco DMV when I was eighteen—another reason for police to shake their heads at me. The clerk put my cell phone and wallet in a plastic bag and took my mug shot. This time I kept my face blank.

My accommodations were Spartan. A metal toilet with no seat or lid. A flickering fluorescent overhead light that stayed on all night. A hard pad and a wool blanket, big enough to cover 60 percent of the length of my body if arranged diagonally, with a corner near my shoulders, and the opposite corner stretched to my ankle-bone. The guard gave me a small meal: half of a shrink-wrapped sandwich of mystery meat with gray bread and a fruit cup—a step up from the school lunches in middle school. I didn't touch the food, but I was fascinated by a bright-orange plastic spork that came with the meal. I figured jails must opt for sporks to trim their utensil budget (fork + spoon = $$; spork = $), and guessed the neon color was to discourage inmates from sneaking them onto the prison yard for shankings. *You'd have to be really committed to gut someone with a spork*, I thought, shivering through a few scattered minutes of sleep. My strongest memory of my night in jail was how cold my feet were. Take away a man's socks and he'll think hard about his life choices.

August 18

The morning of Aunt June's hundredth birthday, a guard gave me an orange jumpsuit, sandals, and, mercifully, a pair of socks. I asked if I might be able to keep the orange spork as a souvenir.

"You don't get souvenirs from jail."

The guard shut the cell door for me to change and I pulled on the baggy suit, tucking the spork into my sock anyway. A minute later the guard came back in to cuff my wrists and ankles and shepherd me into the hallway. I could only shuffle a foot at a time as he led me to the small hearing room, a tiny wood-paneled chamber that barely fit the four of us: myself, the bailiff, the young judge, and the gigantic inmate they sat me down next to. I couldn't believe it—*Tiny*.

Tiny's real name was Ralph Lumley. He was conservatively three hundred pumpkin-like pounds in his bright jumpsuit and shackles—hair oily and stringy, teeth spotted brown, thick green-ish toenails jagged. He'd been, I soon learned, collared for failing to register as a sex offender when he came to Wyoming to work as a traveling carnie. Apparently the state fair was in town and the authorities had rounded up all the pedophiles they could find. Kinder Kids' thicket of barbed wire seemed suddenly sensible.

Ralph and I were slated for a "joint hearing," the judge said—a group trial—which is, apparently, a thing in Wyoming. Lumley's case was up first, and I stared down at his toenails, our elbows grazing, my shoulder rubbing halfway up the armfat spilling into my side of the bench, as the judge read through Ralph's charges and lengthy rap sheet like a grocery list: an assault in Oregon, an indecent exposure in Idaho... When Mr. Lumley got the chance to talk, he described his sad childhood, a broken home, and a drifting life. But he made no excuses and answered the judge's checkbox questions with the boredom of a guy who'd been here many times before. Converse County jail was likely just a quick stop, the judge said with a sigh, in Ralph Lumley's long, upcoming adventure through Wyoming's penal system.

"All right." The judge swiveled his chair around. "You."

Following Lumley, my lame resin-possession story wheezed out like air from a limp balloon.

"You spent the night in jail for *that?*"

Get a weed card back in California, the judge advised me, and kicked me out of his courtroom with a year's unsupervised probation, annoyed his time had been wasted. Wyoming is a funny state—a cop arrests you for a fingernail of crusted pot one day, a judge gives you stoner advice the next. I shuffled out down one hallway to change into my street clothes, and Ralph Lumley shuffled down a different one.

I collected my wallet, phone, change, and receipt for the $1.77 the state of Wyoming had seized during my capture, then wandered down the courtroom steps into the bright frontier sunshine. I called Jackson to update him and blinked down the street, where, just five blocks away, the Wyoming State Fair was, in fact, in full swing. At the carnival I bought myself a ten-gallon hat, a tray of nachos, and a lemonade, then perched on a fence to watch the rodeo, relieved I hadn't become totally hardened on the inside, still able to enjoy the simple pleasure of a crisp jalapeño. It crossed my mind that there were carnies here who might appreciate an update on their friend Ralph, but I didn't ask around.

An hour later I was sitting in a rental car with Jackson and his parents, driving two miles below the speed limit toward Denver. My Subaru was parked at their hotel, where Jackson had stashed the tusk before he and his folks looped back for me. At the Denver Hilton, Jackson and I fought over the dress shirts and ties his parents had brought us, and I reluctantly pulled on the oversize salmon button-down neither of us wanted.

We pulled up to the Pinehurst Country Club thirty minutes before the guests were scheduled to arrive and found Aunt June in the hallway outside the dining room, already annoyed at something or other. She was a short woman with thick gray curls and a slightly rounded spine—clearly old, but lacking the look I associate with one hundred. Aunt June had life to spare and seemed inconvenienced by the celebration—a fuss that could never live up to its hype.

"Aunt June, we were hoping you would take a look at something for us," Jackson gently proposed.

"What is it?" she grumbled.

Jackson unscrewed the top of the black PVC pipe and handed it to her. Aunt June's hand trembled drawing the bone from its sheath. As each spiraled inch of ivory crept out, her frostiness melted, and she started to believe.

"They've done it . . ."

She whispered it at first, then louder and louder—"They've done it. They've done it!"—until she was at a full roar.

"THEY'VE DONE IT!"

Aunt June jigged around the room, tusk raised like Zeus's lightning bolt.

I hadn't met Aunt June until a hundred years in, but on her big birthday, Jackson and I were her dearest friends. Once the other guests showed up, she ferried us around the party by the arm, introducing us as heroes, circling back to us every few minutes to make sure our drinks were freshened. Her rock-hound son, sporting a thin comb-over and high-waisted khakis, gave us a tight-lipped smile—he couldn't congratulate criminals, but he also couldn't offend his mother's most honored guests. At Jackson's dad's request, we didn't tell Aunt June about my night in jail. She didn't approve of drug use—"different times," he said. But I think she would have okayed any act in service of the tusk. I remembered something I'd once heard in a college philosophy class: *What is done for love occurs beyond good and evil.*

On the way out of town, Aunt June invited us over to her suburban house, where she scratched us each a thousand-dollar reward check in shaky cursive, then showed off her collection—petrified redwood chunks, grapefruit-size geodes, mosquitoes trapped in amber—but mostly narwhals—framed watercolors of narwhals, rare books on narwhals, and an empty space in the middle of the dining room table, where her new treasure would rest, in the heart of it all. Before Jackson and I left, Aunt June gave us each a piece of quartz and told us to keep it close, ready always for a challenge.

Back in Mid-City, Jackson and I returned to the couch. I put the check on my desk next to my other souvenirs—my orange spork, quartz nugget and a baggie of narwhal flakes. We called Aunt June a few times to catch up on speakerphone as the months passed, then the years.

As Aunt June's one-hundred-and-second birthday approached, she called Jackson. After being blown away by a recent photo spread in *National Geographic*, he told me, she'd become fascinated by mammoth tusks. She wanted to know how we felt about the Siberian tundra. She figured to do it right we'd have to rent a remote cabin in the winter and wait out the thaw, when ancient ivory starts budding in the Russian icepack. It would be grueling, no doubt, but might just involve a handsome reward for a couple of handsome boys... We laughed. And then we started thinking about how we might pull it off. There's no Craigslist for rural Siberian cabins—we checked. We even looked at dates, but by now our calendars were starting to fill up with work, and it was tougher and tougher to schedule crimes. It was nice to think about, though—miles and miles of snowy wilderness peeling back over the horizon, so far from Mid-City.

Fa Kieu

I'm just . . . worried about you . . ." Mom said through tears at the dining room table when I was fourteen. "What if you end up . . . you know . . . *stealing houses?*"

I thought about the feasibility of this, staring down at the table's soft red cedar, pockmarked and gouged from years of enthusiastic doodling. How would I do it? Pick them clean up off their foundations? Dismantle them brick by brick and rebuild them miles away? Move in when the owners went on vacation and barricade myself inside? It didn't make sense. But after that day's meeting with the police officers at my middle school's office, Mom imagined my sad trajectory: a referral one day, a suspension the next, and before you know it . . . stealing houses.

I made my first walk to the principal's office in kindergarten back when I was Jorge Watsky—just the first of many boneheaded, bizarre, and entirely avoidable delinquencies. Buena Vista elementary, in San Francisco's Potrero Hill District, was a language immersion school, meaning every class was taught in Spanish from the moment Mom and Dad dropped us off on the curb to the moment they picked us up. Classes were small and teachers truly cared about the kids. The only way to make yourself invisible was to speak English.

I'd been sitting cross-legged on the floor for story time one day, my grasp of the language—only a few months into kindergarten—delicate, my attention drifting. Catarina was, like many other Buena Vista teachers, an optimistic, young (but at the time, to me, very old) woman, the tendrils of her unshaved armpits creeping out from her colorful Mexican sundress. The dress fascinated me—the darkness underneath, so vast and mysterious. Everything was bigger then. And after Catarina banished me from class, the hallway swallowed me too, endlessly quiet except for the echo of my footsteps and my pounding heart. The principal reasonably wanted to know what possessed me to crawl under my teacher's skirt.

"¿Por qué, Jorge? ¿Por qué?"

"Because I—"

"Jorge, no," the principal cut me off. *"En español."*

"Quería ver lo que hay ahí abajo."

It was simple: *I wanted to see what's under there.*

Over Christmas break in second grade, my parents sat my brother and me down at the same dining room table at which I would contemplate house-stealing six years later, many of its battle scars yet to appear. Just from the stiff silence in the room, the way they'd staged us across from them, I felt an ominous rot in the pit of my stomach. Secrets hung in the air, consequences waiting to descend on us. I knew this emotion well: the feeling of being called to the principal's office.

We hadn't done anything wrong, they told us. On the contrary, this was fabulous news. They'd found a great new school for us, Alamo, much closer to our Richmond District house.

I hadn't thought of it as anything more than a funny story when I'd told my parents about Buena Vista's recess playground drills—how one whistle meant we were lining up to go back inside, two whistles meant earthquake drill, and three whistles meant to lie flat on your belly on the schoolyard asphalt, separated from the public park on Potrero by a chain-link fence. No kid ever got hit by a stray bullet, but once in a while our teacher's back would stiffen when we heard a loud *pop!* coming from the park.

You'll love Alamo! they insisted. *How could you not, with a school motto like "Be a Friend!" and a mascot like the goofy, grinning Alamo Alligator? Plus, Alamo is a feeder school for Estacada—the top public middle school in the city—and, best of all, everything's already been arranged. You start as soon as Christmas break is over!*

In Cantonese, "Happy New Year!" is *Gung Hay Fat Choy*, "fart" is *fong pei*, and "flower bridge" is *fa kieu*—a classic excuse to get away with saying "fuck you" on the playground. That's all I remember from my Chinese language–learning program, the only class at Alamo with room to take my brother and me midway through second grade. Twice a week we'd study Cantonese and take calligraphy classes, but none of it stuck. Buena Vista had been all over the map ethnically—Mission District Latino kids, black kids, white kids in tie-dye shirts with hippy parents. Maybe it was because we all started out together, or maybe we were just too young to appreciate our differences at Buena Vista. I was an alien at Alamo.

I had a brand-new nickname to replace Jorge—"white boy." It wasn't meant as a compliment. Alamo was so packed with carpet-baggers like me spilling out the windows that they built temporary classroom bungalows on the yard, where I took third grade. Alamo's strengths fueled its budget woes in an ironic cycle: The school was strapped for cash because it was crowded, it was crowded because it was desirable, it was desirable because it was high performing, and, because it was high performing, it was further strapped for cash. Public schools in San Francisco are funded in a need-based system—the schools with the best standardized test scores get the least money. The schools that did the best were heavily Asian, and Alamo, boasting more than a dozen third graders with the last name Wong, was no exception. Kids ate Spam musubi and dry ramen for lunch, sprinkling the powder packets over the noodles and crunching the uncooked chunks like crackers. Monday talk centered around weekend sermons at the local Chinese Presbyterian church. And on Lunar New Year, when we exchanged *Gung Hey Fat Choy*s and kids stacked heavy piles of red and gold envelopes from their grandparents, uncles, and aunts, comparing their little skyscrapers of cash at lunchtime, I stewed in my envy.

Soon after arriving, my brother and I got more good news from our parents—we were getting braces. To be fair, braces aren't a scarlet letter in elementary school. Everyone's got 'em, everyone brags about the *tight* new holiday-themed color scheme of their bands—orange and black (Halloween), green (St. Patrick's Day, duh)—and everyone brags again about how smooth their teeth feel when they come off. But I didn't get standard braces. I got neck gear, a medieval steel rack that curves around the outside of a nerd's overbite and locks into bands around the back molars, ratcheted by a strap that soaks up neck sweat until the padding smells like spoiled cheese. For a few months, through a conspiracy between my parents and orthodontist, I even had to wear the contraption to school. My vintage look included my neck gear, my favorite black snapback hat with its severely bent red brim, and my turtleneck collar, pulled high.

Insecurity takes many forms. It can make a person shrink or put them on the attack; I got loud. I tried to neutralize the barbs by aiming them at myself, anxious that if I didn't cram myself into every silence, someone else might fill it with an insult. I had a seemingly unlimited wealth of annoying insights, and as elementary school dragged on, I was powerless to stop them from escaping the dungeon of my mouth, its orthodontic shackles and oppressive Lunchables breath.

"Actually, it's *octopi*, not *octopuses*."

Third grade was spent propping my arm up at the elbow until Mrs. Luchesi reluctantly called on me. In fourth grade Mr. Gomez was so exasperated he moved my desk into the hallway. In fifth grade I protested Mrs. Avery's rule that only girls could wear hats in class, "in case they have a bad hair day."

"Boys have bad hair days too!" I insisted. "Look!"

Constant hat-wearing and infrequent showering had given me disgusting dandruff, and Mrs. Avery and I found a good rhythm: I'd remove my favorite cap briefly to show her my greasy, matted-down mop, claw at my itchy scalp, send a thick flurry of flakes to my desk, pull my hat back on, she'd demand I remove it, I'd give her some lip, and she'd send me down to Darcy's office.

I remember the view from my seat in front of Principal Darcy Bustamante's desk vividly: the window to the playground over her right shoulder, where light streamed in on sunny days, Ms. Bustamante's hair coiffed in a high blond beehive, her brow furrowed in deep concern, warning me of the slippery slope of misbehavior as I nodded along, daydreaming, studying the framed poster over her left shoulder of a big red apple, popping against a white background, captioned EVERYTHING I NEED TO KNOW I LEARNED IN KINDERGARTEN.

Yeah, right, I thought. *Sell it to Jorge.*

Unlike Alamo's, the principal's office at Estacada Middle School was not designed to make convicts comfortable. There were no scenic views, no cute inspirational posters. Cloudy glass windows latticed with wire honeycomb allowed a trickle of light to complement the unreliable overhead fluorescents. Every object and surface, with the exception of the gray polystyrene ceiling tiles, linoleum flooring, and Principal Lim himself—a slight Chinese man with a thin pencil mustache—was made of the same heavy walnut original to the 1929 building: the door, the room's trim, the chairs, and the massive desk, covered in little nicks and scratches, varnished and revarnished. The principal's desk reminded me of my dining room table, how I could read its history by running my hand over its wounds, imagining nail marks of kids in the thirties clawing at the desk during canings.

Urban public schools don't run on sympathy. I don't think it's a coincidence that Alamo was named after *the* Alamo—the famous Texas fortress—and *estacada* means "stockade" in Spanish. Or that the crop of San Francisco's district middle schools that sprouted in the 1920s share suspiciously similar Spanish colonial revival architecture with the maximum-security San Quentin State Prison across the bay. For most of middle school I got straight As, with the exception of gym class, but I viewed teachers suspiciously. Estacada's a good school as city schools go, but with five hundred kids in each overcrowded grade, and a staff of underpaid, overworked teachers, the system functions through discipline, Ritalin, and respect for authority—anything to keep the school from descending into anarchy.

But I always had to know why: *Why* can't we be on the yard during a free period? *Why* can't I chew gum? *Why* do I have to sing the national anthem? *Why* can't I end a sentence with a preposition—what's that all about? I never got satisfying answers. But whenever the gray intercom wall phone rang in one of my classes, I knew where I was headed.

By middle school, my neck gear, dandruff, and turtleneck were gone, but I tried on whatever version of myself I thought would help me fit in: I played percussion in the orchestra. I rode the bench on the baseball team. I showed up to chess club practice once—the day the yearbook picture was being taken. And I ran for the least competitive student government position available—sixth-grade treasurer—landing on a student council consisting of myself and sixteen Asian girls.

I experimented with weird varieties of jeans—stone-washed and whiskered one month, baggy the next. I bought a pair of huge floppy raver pants at Aéropostale, puffed my navy blue And 1s (puffing is when you pull the laces out of your shoe, roll up a pair of socks and stick them under the tongue to make your feet look like an anime character's), meticulously planned my first-day-of-school outfit (in seventh grade it was all-red nylon pants and a red Old Navy Tech Vest), and tried spiking my hair, the popular look at the time. Straight black Asian hair is perfect for spiking: You just add a layer of gel to the comb, run it through your hair backward, and boom—perfect hedgehog spikes. But Jewy hair doesn't work that way, and more gel just gave me a slimy perm.

Then, in spring of seventh grade came the FUBU debacle. One weekend I took the 5-Fulton bus to a shop on Market Street that sold gaudy, supposedly trendy, extra-baggy Girbaud jeans with red stripes under the knees and functionless diagonal zippers, plus the latest lines from Rhino, Phat Farm, and, of course, FUBU. I knew instantly when I saw it hanging on the rack—the Golden Fleece that would elevate me to high society—a huge baby blue baseball jersey that hung halfway to my knees, FUBU in white cursive across the chest.

I wore the jersey only once before I permanently retired it to my closet, laughed out of homeroom the second I stepped through the door.

Don't you know what FUBU stands for? my classmates marveled.

For Us By Us.

Cheeks burning, I brought the jersey straight to my locker in passing period and wore my undershirt the rest of the day.

It's not totally fair to say I had no friends. There were kids who let me eat lunch with them, who I cracked jokes with in the halls. Bryan Wong, Jeffrey Chu, Oliver Li, and Will Hsiang put up with me as a Kramer who dropped by their bench every once in a while, but they looked down at the floor when I asked if I could go to CUPC, their church summer camp, or if I could try out for Taisho, the Asian youth basketball team they played on. I didn't have real friends—the type you hang out with after school, or talk to about your problems. The type who want to be around you as much as you want to be around them.

But no matter what, I always had Thursday to look forward to. Thursday was Nacho Day, my weekly deliverance from rectangular pizzas so oily they'd cling suctioned to their plastic containers when held upside down. I survived Estacada on a diet of Fritos, Sprite, and anticipation—the faith that Thursday would come again, when the home ec class would set up in the courtyard a period early and heat the cheese vat, and for two fifty I could buy a tray of yellow corn chips drowning in queso, homemade chili, and sliced jalapeños.

Jalepeños were first come, first served, and they went fast. Maybe it's a stubbornness I inherited from my dad—the way he insists that a Papaya King hot dog is incomplete without sauerkraut—but I've always felt passionately that nachos are naked without jalapeños, and I devoted elaborate efforts to getting in line before they ran out.

I might fake sick early on in class, dip out for a bathroom break before the bell, and race to the courtyard. Or maybe I'd skip the period before lunch entirely and accept an absence. Every minute counted with kids queuing up fifteen minutes before the bell, and realistically I had to be no more than sixth in line to get peppers. That's not because public school jalapeños come eighteen to a jar—it's because of backcutting.

Backcutting is one of the most shameful practices known to man. Unlike standard cutting, *back*cutting requires an accomplice in line who allows the cutter to nip in *behind* them. There's a special place in hell for backcut accomplices—gutless suck-ups who shoulder none of the misery they pass on to the chumps after them. The effects of backcutting in a middle school social environment are devastating. I've seen desperate social climbers let five or six popular kids backcut them in a single nacho line, each backcutting cool kid becoming another potential backcut vector, virality taking hold. I've been fourth up, only to see the line's head suddenly bulge like a tumor, thirty-five kids served before me. And I've been kid thirty-five only to see the last jalapeño slice served to kid thirty-four. I've cried in the nacho line. But I've never bent over for a backcutter.

The lunch yard was a tribal wasteland divided by benches: the cool kids—mostly Asian with a smattering of the school's few black, Latino, and the ultra-rare popular white kid mixed in; the FOBs (fresh off the boat—their term of endearment, not mine), wearing exclusively black-and-white clothes and puffed white K-Swiss sneakers; the Russians (not considered white); several varieties of nerds (band nerds, science nerds, theater nerds, although many nerds ate lunch inside); and the AZN Pryde girls (girly-girls who commissioned full-page yearbook spreads for friend groups dubbed "AZN Dragonz," or "The Tiger Lilies"). There was some overlap between the cliques, but mostly their borders were fixed and fiercely guarded.

If there was one bit of glue that held the fractured social world together though, it was hip-hop. We had other cultural bonds—Gap, the mall at Stonestown, the Giants and Niners, Pokémon, Hello Kitty—but no common language was more widely spoken than rap. At Estacada, there were only a few things that reminded us we were all human: When you had control of the radio dial, you turned it to 106.1 FM—hip-hop and R&B on KMEL. And at the end of lunch, when the seagulls perched on the roof swarmed down to fight over our garbage, we were all fighting in the same war, fleeing for cover as bombs dropped around us.

For Christmas in eighth grade, my parents bought me a big black Sony CFD boom box, and for the rest of the year I brought it to school every day, tucking it under my desk when my teachers would allow it in class, propping it up diagonally in my locker when they wouldn't, swinging it through the hallways in every passing period blasting Nelly's "Country Grammar," the first CD I bought from Tower Records on Columbus Avenue, the purchase quickly followed by albums from Mystikal, Eminem, Outkast, Roy Jones Jr., Jadakiss, and Cam'ron. After school I'd watch BET's *106 & Park*, salivating over the weekly Freestyle Friday battles. And that year, when MC Jin, a Chinese-American rapper from Queens who rhymed in a patois of English and Cantonese, won seven straight Freestyle Fridays, becoming the first Asian solo rapper to land a major label deal, Estacada went crazy. I loved the wordplay, the underdogs, and the fact that you could stand up to your enemies by the power of wit. I finally felt as though I'd found myself in hip-hop. But at twelve years old I couldn't separate the lyricism from the lifestyle, and I memorized lyrics about coke dealing, poverty, depraved sex acts, and murder as if they were scripture—worlds far removed from my life, where repercussions for misbehavior were much more permanent than a walk to the principal's office.

I didn't have a lot of public opportunities to showcase my rapping, but there was no better moment to transform an image than a school dance. The day of the spring formal, the DJ, our student council secretary's older cousin, pulled into the parking lot in his Honda Civic, junky spoiler screwed to the body, and grabbed a pair of milk crates from the backseat. He and his friend took turns hauling the box of vinyl singles, belt-drive turntables, crappy mixer, mic, and tangle of cords up the double staircase to the basketball court. And while they were setting up the audio equipment, the student council dance committee girls transformed the smelly run-down gym into a smelly run-down gym disguised with streamers and balloons.

The kids trickled in and the DJs kicked off their carefully constructed set of Top 40 hip-hop and R&B. The cool kids freak-danced at center court, we commoners orbiting around them, boys separated from girls. When the energy peaked, the DJs spun a K-Ci & JoJo slow jam, and the guys on the fringes made beelines for the girls we were crushing on, whose locations in the gym we'd been peripherally tracking all night. I savored the three and a half minutes with Valerie's head resting on my shoulder, her boobs against my chest, until the song ended, we awkwardly parted, and the genders quarantined themselves again.

I made my move right after the slow dance, creeping up non-chalantly while the DJs were distracted. I grabbed the microphone from its resting spot on the folding table and freestyled for as long as I could, rapping in a squeaky pubescent voice over the track vocals to an audience of confused classmates, until the pissed-off DJs slammed my fader down and snatched the mic back. Guerrilla freestyling is like bull-riding. You know you're gonna get thrown off at some point; the victory is in lasting as long as you can. I strutted away into a dance circle, supremely confident that I'd lit the world on fire with my rhymes. But business continued as usual. The cool kids kept on freaking, each twenty minutes the sexes came together for the next slow song, and mostly we stood around, trying not to do anything uncool, our backs stiffening every now and then from a loud *pop!* when some kid stomped on a balloon.

Teachers had to be tough or they'd get walked all over. Kids pounce on weakness. But everyone agreed that Charlie's punishment was cruel and unusual. Asking a thirteen-year-old to pick every piece of gum off the wooden gym floorboards with his fingernails—the caked-in, blackened ones, pounded down by fifteen hundred kids, 180 school days a year (185 if you count dances), every year since the Roosevelt administration—was like giving a man a butter knife to chop down the redwoods.

Mr. Marsden, a slender guy in his early forties, shorts pulled above his knobby pink knees, whistle dangling helplessly from his neck, skeleton keychain rattling on his belt loop, hairline retreating, was a man under siege. He spoke in timid, erratic bursts, piling on perceived troublemakers like a saltshaker whose lid had been unscrewed. It was easy to press Mr. Marsden's buttons, but he had one especially tender spot—a personal shame I never understood: He hated being reminded he was Canadian. But even if I couldn't grasp why it was embarrassing being born north of the border, I could appreciate how a simple statement of fact could be wielded as a weapon. Charlie didn't mean it as a compliment when he called Mr. Marsden a "crazy Canuck" during warm-up stretches one day, and as quickly as Mr. Marsden's face went the color of his flag's maple leaf, Charlie's fate was sealed.

However much Mr. Marsden disliked Charlie, it was dwarfed by his loathing for me. I can't blame him. I was a deadbeat in gym—a perennially tardy back-talker with poor flexibility. But I escaped punishment by exploiting loopholes in the rules. A big part of our grade was based on whether we showed up to class wearing the navy-blue-and-yellow San Francisco Unified School District shirt and shorts. But the rule didn't specify *whose* uniform we had to be wearing, and when I forgot mine at home, I'd raid the big canvas lost-and-found bin in the corner of the locker room and become someone else for the day.

Increasingly, I was Katashi. Katashi Yamada was the most fearsome of the fobsters. High school size after being held back a year for truancy, known for his classic black jacket and jeans, white T-shirt, two long, dangling, bleached-tip bangs, and cutters (baseball batting gloves with the fingers cut off meant to bust an eye open, no relation to backcutters), Katashi was the one kid who all the fake badasses on the yard refused to pick a fight with. One day at lunch, I thought I smelled a *fong pei,* only to realize that Katashi, using his modified disposable lighter with its four-inch-high flame, had lit my hair on fire. I don't think he had anything particularly against me. He was just bored. And he was bored again a couple of weeks later in Mr. Galway's physics class, when, for no particular reason, he decided to squeeze two blocks of dry ice in his hands. Katashi was out of school for the next week with frostbitten fingers, his attendance spottier and spottier as the year dragged on, until eventually he just stopped showing up.

When I discovered Katashi had abandoned his uniform in the lost-and-found, I quit bothering to bring mine to school at all. More and more, I rented his smelly trunks and shirt from the bin, then wore them to class, hitching his massive shorts up every couple of steps during warm-ups, KATASHI YAMADA scrawled across my chest, flashing a shit-eating grin at Mr. Marsden, who, as much as he hated it, couldn't punish me within the rules.

I hobbled toward the end of middle school one Nacho Day at a time, one office visit to the next, carrying my boom box and a tense energy, the righteous indignation of all the rap I'd been listening to, the compensation for my failure to find my place, and a belief that I had within me the power to defeat the enemies keeping me excluded—if only I could figure out who they were. In every moment I was ready for that final challenge, the instant when I would Enter the Wu-Tang, the real me emerging gloriously from a pile of awkward ashes.

So it was in the hallway outside the locker rooms, five minutes before the end-of-gym-class bell on the sunny Friday before eighth-grade spring break, only seven weeks until my release from The Stockade, just algebra class separating me from vacation. Other kids began gathering outside the locker room in their civilian clothes, Mr. Marsden and his whistle blocking the archway to our next classes. I always thought the rule requiring us to stay in gym, even after class had ended, was particularly unfair, and I asked Mr. Marsden to explain the policy.

"*Why*, Mr. Watsky?" he jabbed. "Because the bell hasn't rung yet, that's *why*."

I felt the showdown I'd been waiting for brewing. To the puzzlement of Mr. Marsden, I started fumbling with the buttons on my boom box, cued up "Ride wit Me"—my favorite song on *Country Grammar*—and assumed a hostile stance.

And then I started rapping—at Mr. Marsden—with all the passion I could conjure, as if I could bring his unjust regime to its knees with the power of my punch lines. I have no idea what I said. I can only assume I was regurgitating all the explicit content I'd been consuming and that the rest of the kids scattered around were completely bewildered by the spectacle of a student picking a rap battle with his teacher. I just kept rhyming until the shrill passing-period bell cut me off midsentence, then scrambled away, leaving Mr. Marsden standing there, stunned. Moments later I'd forgotten about the confrontation and headed to algebra class, where, fifteen minutes from the bell that would have delivered me to spring break, the classroom phone rang, and a familiar nausea washed over me.

It was my final visit to Estacada's principal's office.

Threatening the life of a public employee was the official charge. A felony in the state of California, the police officers explained after reading my Miranda rights—serious enough to send me straight to juvenile hall, depending on their mood. I asked where Mr. Marsden was, so I might be able to apologize to him. *Sitting in the next room,* Mr. Lim said, *far too shaken up to see you right now.*

Vice principal Victoria Crowder, Principal Lim, the officers, and my mom brokered a compromise to keep me out of juvenile hall: my name scrubbed from the honor roll, forfeiture of my spot on the eighth-grade trip to Washington, DC, and a five-day suspension that would become an expulsion should I step out of line in the final weeks of school. I wish I could say I had a sense of humor about it at the time, but I was the kind of kid who cried in the nacho line. Beyond being punished by a school I had no respect for, I didn't want to disappoint my mom, who I could see was starting to question whether screwing up wasn't just what I did, but who I was.

"I'm not going to end up stealing houses," I promised her back at home, scanning the old weathered dining room table, remembering years of well-meant sit-downs and talking-tos.

I kept an uncharacteristically low profile when I got back to school from my suspension, and seven Nacho Days later, I was free.

The next year, when I was in high school, I heard Mr. Marsden had been fired from Estacada for scratching a troublemaker he'd caught running in the hall with one of his skeleton keys. It crossed my mind that maybe I'd driven him to the brink of insanity, and this new delinquent was simply the last straw. I think the hurt was deeper in Mr. Marsden's soul, though. Looking back, I see more of myself in him than I would have admitted at the time.

Maybe Mr. Marsden didn't have parents who made him proud to be Canadian or who taught him the difference between rules and fairness. But I hope he did. I hope he was lucky enough to have folks who cared about him as much as mine cared about me. I hope he called his mom up in the Yukon after he got fired from Estacada, and she cried, *Honey, I'm worried aboot you . . . fired for scratching a kid with keys one day, and you'll be stealing hooses the next . . .*

And first he thought about how he'd get away with it, and then it made him want to prove her wrong.

O Positive

The Plaza del Castillo in Pamplona, Spain, was choked with men so drunk and sweaty you could smell the alcohol leaking from their pores. The Chupinazo—the annual kickoff party for the San Fermin festival at the Running of the Bulls—is held in the town square, all the space taken up by hundreds of the type of guys who like to take up space. Every inch of air was a contested armrest—the alphas expanding and the rest of us contorting into the cracks, clinging to lampposts or surrendering to the maelstrom. Not a place for boys, Tim, Robbie, and I agreed—the perfect kickoff for our high school graduation backpacking trip. As we pressed against a stucco apartment building that bordered the vortex, I asked myself what kind of man I was.

When I was younger, I used to imagine with horror the time when there would be no more room on Earth for people. It was inevitable—one day, exponential population growth would hit its limit, each square foot of land crammed with humans—every acre of meadow, mountain, razed forest, and desert at full capacity, all activities occurring standing up: cooking, sleeping, sex, and child-birth, probably performed in a handstand, so that eventually a baby would be blasted up from the seething throng—a child who would become the first member of a new community, a commu-nity who would crawl, and grow, and live on top of the heads of their forebearers beneath them, until the day that new layer over-flowed, too.

In the Chupinazo crowd, so thick all I could see was sky and scalps, my childhood nightmare didn't seem so far-fetched. Every so often a hand, gripping a champagne bottle or a jug of cola, would appear, like an airplane breaching the cloud cover, and a stubbled jaw would tilt back and unhinge. The man attached to the jaw would guzzle as long as he could, before another lurch of the crowd knocked the bottle from his lips, splashing a magenta epaulette across the shoulders of his white shirt. There were burgundy stains everywhere, the aftermath of San Fermin's favorite beverage—kalimotxo—a bastard brew of cola and shitty red wine that demands its drinkers stay eternally hammered, in order to outrun Pamplo-na's notorious hangovers—and bulls.

Spent champagne bottles were simply flung at the cobblestones. And the festival uniform—a fringed red belt tied at the waist, the traditional matching polyester Made-in-China neckerchief, and the stark white linen top and pants—came fitted with a drawstring waist, easy to quickly untie for discreet peeing wherever necessary. I was proud to belong to this staggering, drunk Waldo convention. I took a deep breath and puffed myself full of air.

With our first step off the wall, Robbie, Tim, and I were swept into a riptide, drifting toward the stone gazebo in the center of the square. I pinched a fold of Robbie's shirt between my thumb and forefinger like a mountaineer's rope, glancing down each step to survey the wreckage, navigating cautiously between a puddle of piss and the sharp, smiling fragment of a prosecco bottle.

"Where's Tim?"

Robbie's voice fought to rise above the caterwaul of German, Spanish, and Russian. A cork popped by my right ear. A bottle smashed near my left foot. *Ole, ole, ole ole!* the crowd roared into song. Tim was the biggest of all of us, the alpha-est of our group, and we frantically scanned the belching sea for a head of messy brown hair. Robbie and I yelled ourselves hoarse, but the Pamplona din refused to carry our cries forward. Tim could have been three feet from us or thirty. After a few long minutes, we battled our way through the carwash of elbows toward the edge of the square, where the crowd thinned.

"Tim! Tim!"

I saw his face first, paler than its usual pale, just a few yards away.

"Hey, guys."

Tim swayed side to side, one Jenga brick from collapse. And then I looked down. I didn't notice the blood at first because it matched the belt and bandanna so well, but the white linen of his pants was soaked crimson from his left ankle to knee. All I could see of his left foot was a mess of color and the faint black outline of his sandal thong.

"I don't feel so good."

We draped Tim's arms, Christlike, over our shoulders, and the three of us labored down the nearest alley, past a Catholic church. My Spanish had decayed since the Jorge Watsky days, but I flagged down a stranger to ask for help.

"*Lo siento, donde está . . . ?*" I started.

Wait—el *hospital or* la *hospital?*

I've always had trouble with gender pronouns. When in doubt I go by stereotypes.

Women are healers but men do more stupid shit requiring medical attention . . .

"*¿Donde está* el *hospital?*"

Admittedly it was pretty dumb of us to wear flip-flops. An inch over, the doctor said, and Tim would have severed his dorsalis pedis artery and bled out in ten minutes. We'd beaten the hospital rush—most people don't get injured at the Running of the Bulls until the Running of the Bulls—so they had plenty of spare beds and spare hands to reconnect his tendons.

"I couldn't move my toes at all," Tim bragged, his leg up in traction.

Once it was clear he would survive, the question turned to the next morning's Run. Tim was gonna be laid up in the hospital for days regardless of what Robbie and I did with our time, and we didn't have a strong enough excuse to abandon the mission. I tried to rationalize a way out. We could tell our friends we'd had to stay by Tim's bedside night and day, I figured, wiping his cold sweat and clearing his bedpan. *It was devastating,* I'd say. *We wanted to run so much, but brotherhood prevailed.* Unfortunately, Tim asked us to carry the torch for him.

"Do it. You guys know how much I wanted to run, but . . ."

He gestured to his leg.

Robbie and I set out the next morning in the dark. I cinched my belt above my hip and shifted the pointy tip of my bandanna to the side, to showcase Tim's bloodstain on my chest. The hairs on my arms raised as a chilly breeze snuck under my uniform's thin linen. I don't know if we arrived closer to the beginning or the end of the half-mile route, but even in the first hint of dawn, the course was packed, the horde hemmed in between the city's crowded flats and the gauntlet's makeshift plywood walls. It appeared yesterday's entire Plaza del Castillo crowd had continued drinking since we left, partied through the night, then lurched there, with bottles in hand, barking, tripping, and gagging on their own puke, their belligerence rising in inverse proportion to their coordination. Incredible bravery and incompetence, I marveled: the keys to an early death.

As we took our places on the course, I wondered if there was some way to delay our moment of reckoning. *Should I run with Rob or fend for myself? Press myself up against the wall and wait for the stampede to pass? Jog slow and try to blend into the pack? Sprint to the end of the course and try to duck out an exit?* As the seconds passed, the fuzzy image of myself riding wildly down the course skewered on the horns of a giant mutant bull improved in resolution. I imagined the world a chaotic blur as, whipped around like a rag doll, I looked down to see only a pair of tattered ears, steam puffing through a giant nose ring, and two massive, bloody spikes piercing my body—one poking out my sternum and the other mangling my reproductive organs.

As my pulse quickened and dread deepened, I wondered how it was I could barely stomach the thought of running away from a cow when millions of normal young men through the centuries, all over this world, all over this blood-soaked continent, have marched off to war, prepared to face death and dispense it. What crucial feature must I be lacking? A mental list stacked up quickly: a noble cause . . . the need to protect family and homeland . . . or, in the case of the Old Norse "Berserkers"—the legendary Viking warriors responsible for the phrase *going berserk*, who did battle in a mad, trance-like rage, swinging heavy, hand-forged axes, hacking limbs while plastered and tripping balls—copious amounts of alcohol and hallucinogenic mushrooms.

I even struggled to summon any hatred. I acknowledged the bulls as my enemies, but I knew from the articles I'd read about San Fermin that as I was straightening my bandanna, half a dozen cattle were milling around in a corral at the top of the course being beaten by their handlers, blinded by the jelly rubbed into their eyes, ready to pour out of the gates and barrel into walls, off-balance from the inches sawed off their left horns. They'd pinball into the arena's second holding pen, where the picadors—the men on horses—prepared to lance their backs and necks so that when the fight starts the bulls can't lift their heads to defend themselves against the banderilleros darting around them on foot, pincushioning them with happily colored harpoons, until, by the time the matador finally arrives to wave his cape and swing his shiny blade, the bulls will be so weak and dizzy that a clean death would be merciful. But if the executioner can't find the spinal cord, the animals will be chained by the horns and dragged out of the arena, battered and vaguely conscious while their ears and tail are cut off as trophies and presented to the matador for his heroism.

As Robbie and I straightened our backs for the charge, our impatient comrades became increasingly agitated and started lobbing empty beer bottles over the plywood wall at the police. A few bold runners scaled the fence and belly-flopped into the officers.

And then the gate swung back.

I can't say I've fully experienced a riot, because I never got hit with the club. I just remember a blur of colors—red and white, the navy blue of police button-downs, the gray hair of an old woman, an innocent spectator caught in the crossfire. From what I could tell, no one was seriously hurt, though. We battled the pigs with the same wise strategy brave men employ against bulls—by fleeing.

Robbie and I'd had plenty of practice escaping police in high school. They liked to chase drunk kids through the San Francisco woods on Friday nights. I stayed sober, not because I thought underage drinking was wrong, but because it seemed more social obligation than rebellion, and by high school I was looking for ways to make myself stand out rather than fit in.

One night senior year, after the police broke up an outdoor party at the beer gardens, flashlight beams cutting through the trees, I felt myself kick something small as Robbie and I ran—something that moved. I looked down and saw a baby owl, its right wing twisted, feathers ruffled, hooting gently. We paused and, agreeing we had to take the bird, Robbie scooped it up and carried it as we jogged. When we escaped the park we transferred the puffball into a cardboard box pulled from a Dumpster and looked up veterinary hospitals on our phones, our baby owl peering at us with the shining, black marble eyes of a creature that, so small and vulnerable, it was hard to believe was perched atop the food chain. I proposed we name him Herbert—Herb for short. We hopped the 44-O'Shaughnessy Owl bus (the handful of all-night buses that run in San Francisco are actually, fittingly, called Owl routes) to the Park Animal Hospital, dialed the after-hours phone number on the glass door, and handed Herb to someone better prepared to protect his fragile life.

When Robbie and I stopped sprinting in Pamplona, hands on our knees, we worried only about ourselves.

What do we tell Tim?

Panting, Robbie lifted up the back of his shirt, where the police had planted a foot-long, nightstick-shaped, banana-and-eggplant-colored excuse, sloping steeply from shoulder blade to spine.

"Come! Join me for breakfast, boy!"

A middle-aged man burst from the shutters of his second-story wrought-iron balcony and called down to me in a thick French accent. The early morning sun cast long striping shadows on the sidewalk. Bicycle bells chimed as Paris blinked the sleep from its eyes. I half expected two warbling blue robins to flutter out from behind him and the garbage cans to come to life and break into song. *Does this motherfucker intend to have his way with me, then chop me up for his bouillon?* I wondered.

Paris had been our planned second stop all along. But after Tim's injury, his dad flew from California to France to pick his son up as if it were the end of another school day, and our time in the city turned into a going-away party. I stubbornly lobbied Tim and Robbie to maintain our journey's integrity. *So what if Tim's dad's got money and wants to put us up somewhere with wall sconces and doilies and maids who wear white aprons and shit? This trip is about rugged independence! Making our way without handouts! We won't stay in some sweet, swanky-ass four-star hotel! Right?!*

Tim and Rob shook their heads at me, and we split up after dinner. I could have afforded a hostel, but, intent on proving my manliness, I decided I'd sleep on the street.

After more than an hour of luckless roving through the fifth arrondisement, rejecting stoops for being too small or too exposed, too busy or too isolated, I eventually settled under the archway of a Gothic cathedral, laid down on the top step, tucked the flat side of my backpack under my head, wriggled my arms out of my jacket sleeves and under my shirt, hugging my bare cold arms to my chest, and closed my eyes for what seemed like just a few seconds before the stranger on the balcony was inviting me in for breakfast, and possibly a look at his etchings.

"No, thank you," I insisted three times before he shrugged, shut his windows, and disappeared inside. I suspect he was genuinely kindhearted, eager to share with a street urchin. And my stomach *had* been growling for hours. But there are conversations that I'd rather go hungry for than have with a Frenchman. To explain to him, *No ham for me, sorry—no croissants either—eggs—no, it's not an allergy—I'll pass on the banana, too—yeah, I know, but I just— well, I just don't really like bananas.* I winced, picturing myself as the painfully douchey American houseguest.

A few hours later I lugged my backpack to Tim and Robbie's lovely hotel—whose charms I refused to acknowledge—to prepare for Tim's farewell dinner. I tied my lavender tie in a full Windsor knot—a fact I announced loudly—and pulled on a robin's egg–blue sweater that matched my cuff links but clashed with the hobo identity I was cultivating. Robbie finally had an excuse to wear his wing tips, and Tim wore jeans, a new pair of crutches, and a collared shirt with two buttons open at the top, just like his dad.

"Everything's on me," Andy Somerhill declared that night at dinner. Tim Somerhill's dad is essentially Tim baked in the sun and stretched five inches horizontally in Photoshop. An insurance mogul, he's true to his principles: There's no point living if you're not going to enjoy it, and what a woman doesn't know won't hurt her. I sat across from Mr. Somerhill at the big circular table shared by Tim, Rob, and three or four other friends who happened to be celebrating graduation in Paris. Sitting to my left was Mr. Somerhill's sister-in-law, a multiple divorcée, who I will refer to as Lady Brett Ashley.

"Let me *ask* you something, George," Lady Brett probed me, as we scanned our menus. "What's your blood type?"

"I think I'm O positive," I recalled from a blood drive donation.

"You're *kidding* me. I knew it."

Lady Brett petted my arm, seemingly impressed. Determined not to do anything that might telegraph my nervousness, I left my arm sitting there, her scratching post.

A magnetic force was pulling Lady Brett's pearl necklace down her plunging neckline, across a vast desert of leathery skin that implied too many years tanning on yacht decks off Majorca, Ibiza, Martinique—into the murky deep beyond the fabric of her dress, into the mysterious black abyss that drives men to madness, the shadows between the cliffs of her towering silicone bosom. It was a hex perhaps. I've never liked fake breasts, but Ms. Ashley's necklace yearned downward and my gaze struggled fiercely not to follow.

"And five severed tendons?! How smashed *were* you guys?"

"Actually we were sober," I admitted as she rolled her eyes.

"I mean, we were gonna drink—we just hadn't had time to yet."

"Well, here. Taste my *port*," she offered, pursing her lips and raising a small glass of maroon liquid.

I didn't tell Brett that I'd never been drunk before—that, eighteen and legal in Europe, I'd just had my first adult beverage earlier that week—that all through high school I'd been my crew's voluntary designated driver, shuttling hammered friends home after parties in my mom's used Volvo station wagon.

Port is a classy drink, Brett explained to me, *a dessert wine.*

"But why save dessert for dessert?"

She draped her arm over my shoulder, flicked me playfully on the elbow, and locked her hand in mine, friendlier with every passing glass. At first port had struck me as rich-people kalimotxo, but as we sampled every vintage on the menu, each one tasted better than the last. And the more port I downed, the more my head swam, the more connected I felt to Brett. During a lull in conversation her eyes flitted down to my plate of flaccid vegetables, her brow furrowing. *What was my hang-up?*

"I'm a vegetarian."

"Oh no. No no no no *no!*" Brett insisted. "You're an O positive blood type. That means you're a *leader.* You're extroverted and confident! You *need* meat—"

Lady Brett dipped a spoon in her dish of lamb gravy.

"—to keep your *T levels* up."

She lifted it toward my lips.

"Just a taste . . ."

In four meatless years I hadn't once consciously cheated on my diet. Sure, I'd find out after the fact that some dish had been cooked with chicken stock, or I'd buy a bag of chips with an ambiguous "and natural flavors" on the ingredients list, but nothing like this. Not when I was truly making a choice.

I'm not the tiniest bit sure at all, I thought, *but maybe she's right. Maybe I am confident. Maybe I am a leader. Maybe I should follow whatever this stranger tells me to do . . . Maybe she actually wants to fuck me . . .*

Lady Brett brought the spoon forward with her whole body. And as the lamb crept toward me, Brett's shoulders followed, her dress straps slackening as she bent at the waist, her cleavage pleading for attention, a faint voice in the back of my head begging me not to throw away years of dedication for this temptress whose butt happened to be peeling gradually from its seat, one shapely inch at a time, until the stew was directly underneath my nostrils. Then my bottom lip met the metal spoon, my top lip met the lamb, and I swallowed as fast as I could.

That night was the first time I ever freak-danced with a divorcée. Tim, leg propped up on a chair, was reduced to nursing his drink in the corner while his dad and stepaunt caroused with his friends. *No crutches allowed*, the bouncer at the first discotheque we'd tried had said, shooing us away before we settled for this sweaty, pulsing cave, a bit like the Chupinazo, a bit like a school dance—where the chaperones had decided to fuck off from their jobs and party with the kids.

I figured my only chance with Lady Brett was to wow her with my dancing, so I focused my mental energy on the rhythmic precision of my hips, applying the perfect amount of firm hand pressure to her shoulder blade and lower back, occasionally breaking our embrace to spin her, then draw her right thigh between my legs. *Such talent, such passion, such maturity in the dancing of one so young.* I felt like I was plucking the thoughts directly from her mind, her cheek resting on my shoulder as I kissed her neck. More likely, she was passed out in my arms as I swung her carcass around the room.

"Brett, dance with Robert!" Andy roared, before she peeled herself off me and stumbled away.

Suddenly I was alone, buzz evaporating, in desperate need of a glass of port. There were too many people. I wandered between stumbling clumps of dancers, but every step I took was onto someone's angry toes. I pushed toward the bar through hot blasts of cologne and manfunk, a ghastly thicket of slick-haired French bros crowding me from all sides.

There's a special type of emasculation reserved for the failure to get a bartender's attention. After inching forward from the outer layers, I made it to the bar, where I waited my turn, cracked my knuckles, and waved meekly at servers who looked through me like a ghost to the louder guys who burst up to order dozens of shots and complicated cocktails. Finally, after perhaps weeks, I accepted my drink and smiled toothily at the bartender.

"Merci."

Sipping my sweet wine, watching Robbie rock back and forth with Lady Brett to the blasting Lil Jon, I knew what a true leader would do here.

I have to kill Robbie.

I didn't want to—Rob's a great guy and all—but an alpha male can't be bothered by such trivialities. Fortunately, Ms. Ashley resolved my moral dilemma by leaving the club abruptly—with her sister's husband—and I was excused from murdering my best friend.

I woke up to my first hangover the next morning.

Robbie and I finished the last two weeks of the trip without Tim. We bought a box of joints in Amsterdam, fled a street fight in a fishing village called Hjørring at the tip of Denmark, ferried the fjords in Norway, rode Eurail across Scandinavia, losing all our bags in the process, slept in the Helsinki train station before getting emergency passports issued the next morning, hopped another boat to Germany, and trekked through the Swiss Alps all the way down to

Rome. Ten countries, three weeks, thousands of nubile European girls all around us, and we managed not to get laid once.

My favorite moment was a quiet one, when Rob and I detrained in a random Swedish town after realizing our luggage had been stolen, and wandered in no particular direction until we came across a beautiful, lush lake. We sat on the bank and I pulled out a small cardboard box containing our last prerolled Amsterdam J.

Robbie proposed we name the joint Herb 2.

"Get it, like burnin' *herb?*"

We smoked the joint down to our knuckles, gazing out over the peaceful lake. Sitting there I didn't feel guilty about punking out on the bull-running. The only thing I regretted was letting Lady Brett stick her spoon in my mouth. I wasn't really so interested in the question of what made a man a man anymore—more curious about what made a human a human. Money, recklessness, T levels? A couple of less-manly-sounding words came to mind: intention, serenity, compassion.

I looked over to Robbie, his eyes bloodshot. We would split up in a few weeks and head to different cities for college, but I was thankful for four great years, a good trip, and finally, a real friend.

A person's job is to feel, I thought.

"Man, I feel. Really. Fucking. High."

Our little joint had done its job, too. I rested the roach on a wide leaf and floated it out to the center of the lake, then watched the leaf capsize, the last ember extinguish, and the crutch disappear into the Swedish deep. A Viking funeral for Herb 2.

Down to the Filter

It's easy to hate yourself no matter where you are in the world. But it's especially easy to hate yourself in Los Angeles. You hate yourself because you sit in traffic all day but you never get anywhere. You hate yourself because you're supposed to care deeply about the environment but you're polluting constantly. You hate yourself because everyone else is so beautiful. And beautiful people hate themselves because they know they won't stay beautiful for long. Everyone wants to be young, so if you're not young, you hate yourself. But it takes a lot of long, hard work to be successful, so if you're young, you're probably not successful yet. So you hate yourself for that, unless you're like, Jennifer Lawrence or some shit, and someone as creative as Jennifer Lawrence can probably come up with a reason to hate herself, too. LA's a complicated city, full of lots of different types of people, constantly turning over. Los Angeles breathes, raggedly—it inhales you, exhales you, and, if you're not careful, leaves a nicotine stain on your soul.

For twenty years, Pauly Shore's name has been on the sliding plastic marquee cards of the Comedy Store on Sunset Boulevard. TONIGHT! THE COMEDY STORE, FEATURING: (a revolving cast of trendy stand-ups) AND (always) PAULY SHORE! His parents, who own the club, have never lost faith in their son. They just kept throwing him on stage as he rode his stoner-surfer-bro character up to Hollywood stardom, then down to straight-to-VHS releases, then further down to the college performing circuit, where I met Pauly, in St. Louis in 2010, at a booking conference after party. My agent insisted on walking me across the bar to him, as I begged it wasn't necessary.

"Pauly, I'd like to introduce you to one of my acts—George Watsky. He just finished school and moved out to LA."

I held it together as best I could. This was The Weasel after all. And *Bio-Dome* is an all-time important movie in my life. But I kept it short. The reason guys like Pauly Shore come to these postconference mixers is not to network with eager young actors hoping to further displace them in the industry, but to find someone to bring back to their hotel room. He was nicer than he had to be, though. He gave me his email address and told me he'd be happy to link up in Los Angeles, and we shook hands, knowing that we never would.

In February 2010, Jackson and I had just moved into a temporary apartment complex in Burbank. At first glance, the Oakwood Apartments, equipped with new cookie-cutter beds and couches, working refrigerators, strong water pressure, ample parking, clean carpets, and just four blocks from In-N-Out, are great. But by the end of the first month, the community's creepy underbelly started to show.

One Wednesday in March, we were hanging out in the living room when sirens filled the air. You hear ambulances all the time living in a city, but this was different. The wailing got closer and closer until it was just a building away, not just one ambulance, but rather a howling choir, chopped with the whir of helicopter blades. I connected the dots the next day when the tabloid story broke—featuring an overhead photograph of our new apartment—that the ambulances were for the ex-dimple-cheeked-teen-heartthrob Corey Haim. Recent years hadn't gone well for Corey, and he fatally overdosed a unit over from where Jackson and I had just unpacked our first California boxes.

Each day, right where the medics had pulled up, packs of nauseatingly cute aspiring child stars, in town for pilot season, roamed the parking lots like feral dogs. If they took classes at all, they were enrolled in "industry-friendly" schools, or, more accurately, industry-friendly "schools." You'd see them by the pool breaking curfew, smoking menthols—unchaperoned twelve-year-olds with perfectly spiked hair and whitened smiles, discussing their career visions.

"See this green wristband—that's gonna be my *signature*."

We were five minutes from a bunch of major Hollywood entry points. The Warner Bros. and Disney lots were just up Barham Boulevard, plus Vivid Entertainment, right across the 101, if all else failed. The Oakwoods' affordable, furnished, month-to-month rooms were perfect for both child actors and addicts caught in a downward spiral. It wasn't just Corey Haim—Rick James headlines a star-studded class of entertainers who drew their last breath at the Oakwoods.

I imagined the coroners carrying Corey's body bag out to the final chauffeur, right before the apartment staff trashed his framed cast photos and takeout containers, wiped down the surfaces, Febrezed, then handed the keys over to the next smiling family from Houston or Indianapolis. It didn't take long to figure out what the Oakwood Apartments really are: holding cells for people on the way into show business—or on the way out.

I wish I could completely distance myself from what the Oakwoods represent, but I wasn't there by accident. I didn't start auditioning until a few months later, when Jackson and I signed a real lease in Mid-City. But soon enough, I was sitting in the same waiting rooms as, if not the Oakwoods kids, the slightly older versions of them, clutching my glossy headshot and highlighted script sides, trying to sit up straight, whispering my lines under my breath.

"You feeling better?"

"You feeling *better*?"

"You . . . *feeling* better?

On my very first audition in Los Angeles I was winnowed down to the final three choices for the lead role in a major studio feature film called Project X. I didn't get the part, but I brushed off the rejection—if I came that close on my first audition, I figured this whole stardom thing was gonna be quick.

I never came that close again.

The general rule is, the more degrading the role, the easier to land. Six months after moving to LA I was striking out on everything. Striking out on nerdy-best-friend-corny-sitcom parts. Striking out on one-line pizza delivery guy roles. Striking out on Internet-only commercials looking for "real dog lovers." My principles started to fray around the edges. A new actor who turns their nose up at parts doesn't inspire a lot of confidence from their agents, and the list of companies in whose commercials I would have gladly appeared were limited to the San Francisco Giants, Volvo, and my dad's therapy practice.

But I didn't have the luxury of morals. At least that's the logic I used to rationalize auditioning for a Kentucky Fried Chicken commercial one week and a People for the Ethical Treatment of Animals ad the next. I whiffed for KFC. But I got a callback for PETA—my first in months. And when I made it to the final round for the lead part, I was so relieved to be in the mix I conveniently overlooked the fact that PETA sucks. That this was the ad department that rolled out such lovely campaigns as the YOUR MOMMY KILLS ANIMALS! series, featuring a sadistic housewife covered in blood, gutting a bunny with a butcher knife; the TO ANIMALS, ALL PEOPLE ARE NAZIS ads; a million sexually suggestive billboards featuring models and porn stars; and the unforgivable ANIMALS CAN MAKE U SMILE poster, featuring Justin Bieber.

None of that mattered now that I'd made it to the coveted final callback. To get to this point an actor must advance through a draining obstacle course, starting with the preliminary read, where, after waiting hours in a tiny, windowless room crammed with your doppelgangers, you get a crack at a five-minute taped session with a casting assistant. The few who make it beyond the hundreds in the cattle call to the first callback with the casting director, then past the second callback with the director, arrive here, at the final callback—the chemistry read—which gauges your electricity with potential scene partners and ultimately your ability to pitch the client's shitty product to the masses.

Since I'd gotten this close to landing the PETA part, it follows that the role was somehow humiliating. The little red button on top of the camera blinked as I peeled off my T-shirt, a panel of producers jotting notes about my specific shade of paleness and areola diameter. I studied the ground as my scene partner, a beautiful, blond twentysomething reading the role of "Jessica," shyly removed her loose sweater and strapped on her neck brace prop.

"I'll read the voiceover narration," the casting director offered cheerfully.

"Any questions about the material?"

Jessica looked over to me in her foam brace and gray bra, and we shook our heads timidly.

"No? Okay, let's give it a shot!"

I patched the huge imaginary hole in the imaginary wall with my imaginary spackler, as per the script, smoothing out the edges of the invisible plaster enthusiastically, my endangered acting career resting on the quality of my pretend carpentry.

"This is Jessica," the casting director smirked slyly. "She suffers from 'B.W.V.A.K.T.-BOOM!—Boyfriend Went Vegan and Knocked the Bottom Out of Me,' a painful condition that occurs when boyfriends go vegan and can suddenly bring it like a *tantric porn star.*"

I cleared my throat for my only line.

"Oh, you're *back*—you feeling better?" I asked Jessica, in the deepest tone of concern I could muster, immediately certain I'd botched the emphasis. Jessica, the star of the commercial, shrugged dramatically, a flair she added on her own. And that was it. The characterization of the shrug was Jessica's only opportunity to wow the panel with her acting chops, since she didn't, technically, have any lines. The commercial would include, however, a flashback shot of her being taken from behind, presumably right before her head smashes through the wall.

"Good," the casting director said. "Let's play around with it."

We ran the scene again, and I patched a new hole with startling conviction—the hole was real, it occurred to me—it was just the wall around the hole that was missing. Jessica nailed her shrug, we groggily put our clothes back on, and casting called in the next hungry couple. For the next few days I brought my phone with me to the bathroom in case my big break came while I was peeing.

Apparently I'm a good pretend spackler.

"You're on hold!" my manager, Ted, excitedly told me.

(Being "on hold" is when a producer offers a shortlisted actor the privilege of clearing their schedule for a part they still haven't landed.)

"But," Ted confided to me, "casting says you're in."

It didn't matter that I would be playing a dweeb in a commercial for a despised organization—a commercial that hinged on a weird joke about sexual violence and the dubious assumption that everyone wants to screw a vegan. What was important was that I'd gotten the part. I was taking my first step toward Hollywood superstardom, and it was time to start living the lifestyle. So I celebrated like any new Los Angelino cast in their first PETA spot would.

"Just snort it fast," Reggie said, edging the coke with his credit card. I'd asked him for a beginner's line, this being my first time.

It's mostly a coincidence that I ended up in Las Vegas that weekend. I don't like Las Vegas. It's the PETA of cities. Plus I suck at cards. But the Golden Nugget had awarded Reggie a free room for customer loyalty, so six of us ironed our best vertically striped shirts, piled into one hatchback, and spent the ride up the 15 arguing over which *Entourage* character we each represented.

At the hotel room, Reggie handed me two cans of Four Loko, an energy drink–vodka cocktail so strong the state legislature had just banned it due to reports, Reggie insisted, of people in comas or with exploded hearts.

"This was the last original batch before they had to water down the formula."

The last thing I remember that night was looking out over the glittering lights of the manufactured desert city from the balcony of Ghostbar, then deciding that I didn't want to be there anymore, and drifting out the door alone.

I woke up facedown on the hotel room floor, drool dripping from my mouth and pooling on the carpet, its pattern pressed into

my cheek. A bright slice of sunlight snuck out the side of the drawn
blackout curtains, my snoring friends draped over every piece of
furniture. My brain throbbed. I groaned, wondering why my
knees and shins ached so badly. And then the night came back to
me in fleeting patches: walking and walking and walking aim-
lessly, shivering, tucking my arms inside my T-shirt, cursing out a
security guard guilty only of trying to help me find my way back
to the hotel, and the blaring of car horns as I Froggered across the
Vegas strip on foot.

I propped myself up on an elbow and scrolled through last
night's illegible text messages, trying to reconstruct the evening.

"eher r u go home"

"I left"

"yes heo? Rm #?"

Then my email buzzed with an unopened message from Ted.

"They went with the other kid."

I pressed my face back into the carpet.

I needed a spa day. Jackson and I never really thought much about
City Spa, the dilapidated sauna on our block, kitty-corner to Kinder
Kids, its paint job fading, a few tiles missing from its terracotta
awning. It was only half a block from our house, but it never crossed
our minds to actually go inside. We'd speculated, since we never
actually saw any customers, that it might be a brothel or a shell business for a money-laundering operation. But that weekend we decided
to soothe our corroded Hollywood souls with a boys' day at the spa.

Up until this point in my life I had generally avoided being naked around other guys. I never went to a school with group showers, and in middle school I was so paranoid of being pantsed—or worse, underpantsed—that I wore two pairs of underwear beneath my gym shorts: boxers on top, tighty-whities on the bottom. It was the safest way to navigate the locker room, plus I got the pleasant support of briefs with the fashion flair of boxers. But today I was committed to making some life changes. Jackson, our friends Kush, Vito, Phil, and I marched in the front door confidently.

It's a tradition for LA businesses to have a wall of signed headshots behind the cash register. Delis, Laundromats, and liquor stores proudly display a monument to their celebrity clientele. Walls they've curated over decades of business, featuring photos of A-listers sprinkled in with eighties soap opera stars whose careers have long since hit the rocks but who still have dry cleaning needs. *Mid-Wilshire Liquor—Liquor store to the stars!* they advertise, from which we're supposed to reason, *Well, if Pat Sajak buys his Captain Morgan here, it's good enough for me.*

The City Spa on Burnside and Pico has such a wall, but it features a single photograph: Pauly Shore.

"Crazy, I met him last week in St. Louis," I informed my friends as we collected our towels and locker keys. They grunted. Nobody likes a name-dropper.

The lobby of City Spa was spare, concrete-floored, and empty, except for the attendant and us. But when we pushed through the swinging door to the locker room we were smacked with humidity and loud Greek and Russian chatter. Sweaty, spherical, middle-aged, and elderly men strutted around, some with towels around their wastes, some naked, their pregnant-looking guts obscuring their genitals. Seeing the crowd, I felt suddenly sleek and sexy and my shoulders relaxed. The six of us stripped with varying degrees of cheerfulness as Jackson whipped Kush with a birch leaf.

The most exposed portion of a City Spa day is the thirty-yard walk to and from the locker room to the pool area, and long after the rest of the guys had hit the hot tub, I was still anxiously fiddling with my towel by the showers.

One of the first assignments in my 101 college acting class was to walk across the room. That's it. Just walk, from one end to the other, the rest of the class watching. The idea was that with so many eyeballs on you, you'd be forced to pay attention to every minute detail of an act we take for granted. How far do you bring your shoulders back? How does the weight transfer from the heel of the foot to the ball? How fast are your footsteps? How heavy? What the hell do you do with your hands? And how can you act like no one's watching when you know that everyone is?

I thought back to acting class, put one foot in front of the other, and before I knew it I was in the hot tub, under the bubbles and laughing with everyone, all my stress for nothing. After a colossal Russian guy got tired of us and heaved himself out, the water level sank four inches and we had the tub to ourselves.

And then a shadowy figure knifed surgically into the water. Before I ever saw him walking up, he was sitting there, arms resting casually against the lip of the tub, directly across the bubbles from me. *No fucking way,* I thought.

"Pauly Shore?!"

I couldn't help but blurt it out. Pauly didn't even have to turn his head to look at me, just shift his gaze a couple of ticks. His expression barely changed, but a tiny downturn of his eyebrows admonished, *You should know better than to bother me*, a tiny upturn of his lips acknowledged, *That's me, all right—Pauly Fucking Shore.*

"We met in St. Louis a couple weeks ago at the booking conference. I have your email address."

"Oh. Yeah. Right on."

It seemed to disappoint him that we'd already met. It meant he wasn't being bugged by a fan, although I wish I could have reassured him that I *was* a fan and would have bugged him regardless. I didn't want to make Pauly Shore sad. Just like in St. Louis, he was nice enough to chat with me for a few minutes.

"This is my Zen place," he said. "It's the only place that I can come to clear my mind from all the craziness."

I was awestruck. Pauly Shore legitimately loved the crappy Russian bathhouse on my corner. I could tell he didn't want to have a long discussion, so I rejoined my friends' conversation, dropping in a "yeah" or a "for sure" every now and then, still hyperaware of Pauly looming across the hot tub.

It dawned on me that one of us was going to have to get out first. Either Pauly was going to see me naked or I was going to see him. I felt sick. I hadn't planned on my self-acceptance course moving that fast. But I couldn't freeze out The Weasel. This was a man who'd lived his whole life under a public microscope. Who had seen the highs and the lows, the adulation and the humiliation, and soldiered on. *I won't force Pauly Shore into yet another compromising position,* I thought. *Not in his Zen place.*

I decided I would leave the tub first. I would conquer my hang-ups, present myself proudly, and say, *This is who I am, Pauly, and today, I choose to love myself.*

And so I sopped out of the water and nodded good-bye to The Weasel. I stood at the tub's edge a few seconds longer than I had to, while the droplets ran off me, so he would know I was not ashamed. And I walked over to the pool calmly, one foot at a time, my heels deferring gracefully to the balls of my feet, my shoulders relaxed, my head held high, my spine long, feeling as though I had both the eyes of the world on me and no one's at all.

Then, a minute or so after I'd lowered myself into the chlorine, I saw Pauly start to lift himself from the hot tub. I couldn't help but peek. From the corner of my eye I watched that bastard walk out of the room wearing an American flag Speedo. And while the rest of us pruned up in each other's filth, exposed, Pauly—I'm sure—winked at his headshot while he strolled out the doors of City Spa, whistling, back into the thick LA smog, a survivor.

Ask Me What I'm Doing Tonight!

The remodeled University of North Dakota student center was tastefully lit, set up like a game room, with a dartboard and convincing synthetic "hardwood" floors, snowflakes dusting the Grand Forks streets outside. Five minutes before showtime in the winter of 2008, there were exactly zero people in the room. Well, I was there, and counting the student activities committee, there were *exactly* four of us—plus the two kids playing pool in the corner—but they'd already said they didn't like poetry, to which, in that moment, I nodded in quiet agreement

I'm sorry . . . we really did try to promote the show. It's a tough Saturday—home football game. Plus it's the first weekend of deer hunting season, so a lot of kids are off campus . . . come to think of it, why did we book a show this weekend?

In the five years I spent doing spoken word on the college circuit, I played 193 campus gigs. It was always roughly the same routine: Wednesday night I'd print out my contracts for the three weekend shows, staple them to my flight itinerary, and write the student contact phone number onto each sheet. Thursday morning I'd leave my house in Jamaica Plain while it was still dark out with my backpack, a pillow, and carry-on, walk to the Green Street station for the 5:00 A.M. Orange Line metro, transfer at Chinatown to the Red Line, transfer again at Downtown Crossing to the Silver Line bus, and ride it to Boston Logan. I'd check in for a flight leaving around 7:30 for Minneapolis, or Chicago, or Charlotte, Denver, Seattle, or Atlanta. I'd sit in a window seat with my pillow, fall asleep as soon as I sat down, and wake up when our wheels hit the ground. I'd rent an economy car at Thrifty, or Budget, or Enterprise, and drive to wherever my Thursday-night gig was. If I had time, I'd check into my room and drop my bag at Motel 6, or the Red Roof Inn, or La Quinta Inn and Suites. Then I'd drive to campus and meet the kids on the student activities committee, wearing matching T-shirts with slogans like "CAB," "APB," or "ASK ME WHAT I'M DOING TONIGHT!," whom I would never see again for the rest of my life, and we'd talk about that awful rainstorm that just passed, or that awful snowstorm on the way, until showtime. Afterward, I'd get back in my rental car, stop at Walmart and pick up some emotional crutches—maybe a box of Stouffer's mac and cheese and a Coke—drive back to my Motel 6, or Red Roof, or La Quinta Inn and Suites, watch *The Daily Show*, microwave my macaroni, chug my Coke, then fall asleep without brushing my teeth.

During that time, I learned there's a Manhattan in Kansas—

they call themselves the Little Apple, and they love it when you talk shit about the Jayhawks, but if you have a show the next night at KU, a jab about the Wildcats is gonna help you with the crowd. I learned Casey's General Store is not a general store, it's just a gas station that sells shitty pizza, and the best thing about Kum & Go truck stops is the name. At the A&Ws in Minnesota, Wisconsin, and northern Iowa you can get fried cheese curds with your shake, and at any gas station you can get raw curds—the kind that squeak between your teeth. There are nights in Minnesota where it's so cold that the boogers crystalize in your nose the second you step out of your car. Cedar Rapids, Iowa, is not to be confused with Cedar Falls, Iowa, which is not to be confused with Cedar Falls, Wisconsin, and Sioux City, Iowa, is not to be confused with Sioux Falls, South Dakota. There's even a Sioux Rapids in Iowa, but it doesn't have any colleges. I learned that Sioux City, Iowa, smells like manure because of the Tyson Foods slaughterhouse, but Cedar Rapids, Iowa, is the "City of Five Smells" because of the General Mills factory—the morning breeze might be scented like Cocoa Puffs or Cheerios, but when the wind changes it's rotten eggs.

I remember Salina, Kansas. An hour outside of Manhattan, Salina's just big enough to have its own water tower. At the center of town, the H. D. Lee flour mill's rusty steel sign trellis still crowns its abandoned brick granaries, isolated from the rest of the town by a chain-link fence. Two pizza joints remain open on Main Street, but the only businesses that seem to be thriving are the bars and the Methodist church, its stone fresco engraved with HE WHO

DOES NOT TAKE UP HIS CROSS AND FOLLOW IS NOT WORTHY OF ME.
Mostly the town's a graveyard of closed storefronts, sun-bleached
awnings, and FOR LEASE signs pockmarking the empty windows.
You could do three laps around the block in the middle of the day
without seeing another pedestrian. On the outskirts of town, the
water tower still reads SALINA, KANSAS: RIGHT PLACE. RIGHT REA-
SON. RIGHT NOW, a slogan someone came up with a long time ago.

Salina is not unique. Main Street looks the same in so many of
the rural towns that dot the Midwest, separated by hundreds of
miles of square plots sprinkled with barns and silos: a post office, a
coffee shop, an antique store, a Methodist church, a Lutheran
church, a Catholic church, three or four bars, a Chinese restaurant, and a whole bunch of vacant storefronts—faded pages from a
previous draft of America.

Usually the motels I stayed at were a few miles outside of town,
sharing a shopping complex off the freeway with a McDonald's, a
Panera, and a Rite Aid. The day I checked into my Motel 6 near
Manhattan, the local headlines mourned a teenager who'd died in
a wheat avalanche when the shelf of seed above him collapsed.
One of the most dangerous jobs at the granary, I learned from the
article, is to knock down the wheat stuck to the silo ceiling. Work-
ers tried to shovel down to him, but by the time they pulled his
body out of the seed, he'd suffocated under his product.

And here I was with my wheelie suitcase, arrived from Boston to
make sense of life's bitter ironies. Midwestern kids study for all the
same useless degrees as kids in New York and Boston—philosophy,
dance performance, art history—but a lot of them take paths coastal

kids wouldn't consider, like agriculture and animal husbandry. *How would I connect with someone who was going to spend the rest of their life analyzing crop yields or with their gloved hand up a cow's vagina?* Sure, love poems will never go out of style. But the material that worked best—from Appleton, Wisconsin, to Minot, North Dakota—was pop culture.

When I started playing the college circuit in 2007, the most consistent laugh line in my set was a joke about Alanis Morissette. But three years later, no one was laughing. *Did these kids finally realize the poem sucks?* I wondered. At the next show, I swapped Britney Spears for Alanis without changing any other lines, and suddenly everyone was laughing again. Then, two more years passed and the new crop of college kids no longer found Britney Spears amusing. At the tail end of my time on the campus circuit, I traded Britney Spears for One Direction, and I was funny again. Two celebrities had managed to become irrelevant while I kept circling the plains. I knew the references didn't make my poems good. But celebrity gossip is like sports, or the weather: cheap Elmer's glue for people who can't figure out another way to bond.

Even pop culture references are useless if no one shows up. Laughter is contagious—you need victims to spread it, and with too much empty space, jokes die fast. In playing a show for a tiny group of people, there are actually two performances going on—your performance to the audience, and the audience's performance back to you. A lot of small crowds will sit stone-faced, but the kindhearted ones will fake a laugh—a humane act that keeps journeymen performers from blowing their brains out in Super 8 bathrooms.

I'd performed a lot of dud college gigs by the time I hit University of North Dakota. Shows for a dozen indifferent college kids, the espresso machine louder than me, afternoon lunchtime shows at technical community colleges, half the audience playing *Warcraft* on their laptops. But UND was the first school where literally *no one* showed up. It was actually a relief. Sure, it's embarrassing to fly two-thirds of the way across the country, drive another 350 miles alone in a rental car, collect a check for doing nothing, and go back to the motel. But it beats the awkwardness of performing for five people for an entire hour, as the contract requires.

The campus board and I waited in the student center until the show's start time passed. Then we waited another five minutes, to be sure. And then, as I was about to leave, three students walked through the door.

"Oh great! We can still do the show!"

I was a cornered animal. The student organizers dragged three lounge chairs into the middle of the room and arranged them in a semicircle, each chair separated by five barren feet. They were big, throne-like recliners, the kind that take your arms far away from your body when you lay them on the wide armrests. The left and right chairs hemmed me in from either side, while the middle chair aimed straight at me, dead center.

The next morning I drove back down from Grand Forks to Minneapolis, feeling incredibly out of touch. I passed one pickup truck after another carrying beautiful, silent deer strapped to the beds—

bucks with big antler racks, patches of white and golden fur, and the same glassy eyes as yesterday's audience—followed, a few miles down the freeway, by a towering, giggling baby plastered on a billboard, captioned I COULD SMILE BEFORE I WAS BORN!

But a few months later my show in Kirksville, Missouri, was packed, students sitting cross-legged, feet dangling from the balcony of the Truman State student lounge. My newly introduced Britney Spears line killed. And so did all the other lines, even the ones that didn't rely on pop culture, swells of laughter rising and falling just where I intended, silences between lines complete, the crowd following every word. My nerves melted and so did theirs—their concern that I might embarrass myself—and neither of us were performing for each other anymore, just listening and reacting. I had no reason to expect this town to be any better than Grand Forks, to think that I should be able to connect with the kids in Kirksville, Missouri, but I had no reason not to, and I'd learned after this many shows that any single performance can be the one that inflates your ego or destroys it, the night that makes you feel like a big web of energy links every single being across time and space, or the gig that alienates you from every shallow, shitty human on the planet.

After the show, I rolled around in a field with a pretty redheaded agricultural engineering student, like I got to do occasionally after good gigs. We pulled ourselves apart and lay on our backs, looking up at the quilt of stars, hundreds of miles from the light pollution of St. Louis.

"Am I going to see you again?"

"Yes."

I never really gave much thought to the fields while flying over them. It just seems like a whole lot of empty space from above, but I wonder how many half-naked kids you'd see rolling around in them if you zoomed in.

Back at the Super 8 I scraped the golden, crusty cheese off the corners of my Stouffer's container with a plastic fork I'd picked up at the front desk. The corners are the best part, and I always save them for last. *Maybe I'll start eating better on the road,* I thought, and checked the ingredients on the back of the Stouffer's box.

"Wheat."

But maybe later.

Crying & Baseball

"Fairness" is when you get what you want.

—My dad, presumably joking

More than the apartment's musty mothball smell, more than the metallic taste of the drinking water Grandma insisted on boiling, and even more than the seventeenth-century gold-leaf chamber pot in the corner of the living room, I was fascinated by the mysterious disappearance of the entire thirteenth story of Grandma's apartment building. All the other floors were perfectly intact, down to the basement. But the elevator buttons skipped straight from 12 to 14 without a hiccup. *Isn't anybody alarmed about this?* I asked my dad. *How could New Yorkers, who haggle over every nickel at the dry cleaners, quietly let a dozen apartments and their tenants disappear into an alternate universe?*

"The fourteenth floor is really just the thirteenth floor," Dad explained to me. "They just call it the fourteenth because thirteen is an unlucky number and nobody would want to live on the thirteenth floor."

"But they *still live* on the thirteenth floor. They just *call* it something different. They're lying."

"Maybe, but it makes them feel better. There's an old religious belief in something called the Evil Eye—sort of . . . the gaze of God. If you draw the Evil Eye's attention, you're asking to be punished."

"Why is thirteen unlucky?" I asked.

"I don't know. It's tradition."

My dad, Paul Norman Watsky, was born on Friday, the thirteenth, the most traditionally unlucky day of them all.

In 1955, Dad was an unathletic twelve-year-old, lingering at the window of his family's Manhattan apartment, staring down at the beehive below, asking himself if he had the nerve to dive into the frenzy of Yellow Cabs, questioning whether a body bounces or crunches, debating the merits of feetfirst or headfirst, and wondering if his mother would finally admit her mistakes if he did it—if she would apologize for the intimidation and pressure and the way she manipulated his father to make him shrink into himself. He doubted it.

I remember Grandma Syde as a fearful woman—fearful of death, of danger, of anyone who wasn't Jewish, of being unloved. Raised in poverty in New York, she lived her young adulthood in the Great Depression, and until the end she'd have you check that the coast was clear at restaurants before wrapping the extra dinner rolls and butter pats in a napkin and sneaking them into her purse. But for my dad growing up an only child—the only person she had total power over—she swung between belittlement and sugary praise, attempting to keep him weak and dependent, another commodity to be contained, wrapped up, and hoarded in her purse.

Dad will tell you Dr. Luloff saved his life. Harry Luloff wasn't a physically impressive man—not even to a twelve-year-old. A Freudian analyst, he was a balding, middle-aged chain-smoker who dressed in short-sleeve white button-downs. And he was low-key—so low-key that he was willing to put up with Dad's muteness for the first two years of sessions, letting his patient spend their time building model boats and airplanes to bring home and destroy, until Dad finally got comfortable and started talking. After Dad rejected—or was rejected by—six other potential candidates, Dr. Luloff clicked. It wasn't so much what he did, but what he didn't.

"He was the first grownup who I ever felt didn't want something from me," my dad once told me.

By the time Dad was as undergrad at NYU, he and Dr. Luloff had tapered from three, down to one consultation a week. Dad wasn't fantasizing about throwing himself from windows anymore, but it was still a slow process figuring out kids his age. One lonely summer, when Dad was dragging himself through a job in the Reynolds & Co. mailroom, surrounded by blue-collar guys he could only assume hated him, Dr. Luloff made a suggestion:

"Read the sports page."

It was unwelcome advice. Sports were a useless diversion, Dad thought, the opiate of the masses, invented to get sheep to flush their money down the toilet. But Dr. Luloff persisted. The strategy reeked of desperation, but Dad was desperate. Summer in New York was all about baseball, and one night before work, he checked the scores in *The Times.*

It worked. Dad offered a comment on the game and the guys included him. And with every shared smile over a win or obscenity over a loss, he suggested to the other guys in the mailroom that *maybe Paul's not on a completely different planet.* But Dad had created a new problem: He'd now established himself in the mailroom as a baseball guy, and reading the sports page once wasn't good enough. If he wanted to maintain the charade, he had to *keep* reading.

Something bizarre started happening. My dad began opening the sports page by habit. He dug into the history, the narratives, and imagery of the game. He developed favorite players. He started to care who won and lost. It was weird. Dad accidentally liked baseball.

That summer, the '62 Yankees, led by Yogi Berra, Mickey Mantle, and Roger Maris, played Willie Mays and the San Francisco Giants, who'd just moved west from New York, in the World Series. After a huge storm in California delayed the series for four days, the Yankees won the game seven clincher 1–0 at Candlestick Park, when Willie McCovey famously smashed a line drive, with two outs in the bottom of the ninth inning, runners on second and third, straight into Yankees second baseman Bobby Richardson's glove. New York went nuts, but Dad would have been happy either way. He still liked the Giants.

My dad was thirty when he met his first best friend, in 1974. The year had gotten off to a rocky start. After following the Giants west, Dad was fired from his five-year professorship at SF State over friction with the school administration. He was still hurting when an old student called him. The kid wanted to know: would (ex)Professor Watsky change his grade from an incomplete to a pass if he finally submitted his years-late final project? And could he turn in some poems instead of the actual project? It didn't make much sense, Dad recalled to me, going out of his way to accommodate a lazy former student from a school he no longer worked for. But he asked where to meet the guy anyway and headed to Salus House in San Francisco. Dad recognized the name "Salus House"—a Jungian mental health group treatment home—an alternative to hospitalization and medication for young, first-break schizophrenics. He hadn't been aware of his former student's condition, but the two of them sat, backs against the wall, on the pillows and rugs of an otherwise unfurnished Salus House room, trading poetry back and forth, when a fuzzy-haired clinician walked in.

"You have to leave," the employee ordered, before softening and asking Dad what he was doing.

"We're reading poetry," Dad explained.

"Well, if you're not a family member, you can't stay for dinner."

But the clinician decided to sit and listen for a while. And a little bit later, he changed his mind, introduced himself as Saul, and invited Dad to stay and eat.

Standing on opposite sides of the introvert/extrovert rift, my dad and Saul didn't make for obvious best friends.

"Once Saul was telling me about his Sunday," my dad explained it me. "Saul said *incredible*. He'd been to parties in San Jose, Oakland, and San Francisco—mingling in every corner of the Bay Area on the same day. I just shook my head and said, *Saul, I can't imagine anything more horrible.*"

But they had more to bond them than to separate them. There were the obvious surface similarities: both New York natives, Giants fans, and Jews (Dad, vaguely, Saul, emphatically); but also a pain they both understood in each other: burdens they'd been carrying their whole lives from poisonous mothers and passive fathers; and a belief in alchemy: that they could turn that pain into something productive.

It didn't take long for Saul to talk Dad into joining him in psychology school. Carl Jung's ideas resonated with my father—the concept of the Wounded Healer—that a psychologist isn't a robot with a notepad, but rather another human being, damaged and empathetic, whose trauma can form a bridge to their patients. Despite their shared careers, I don't remember ever hearing Dad and Saul talk about psychology. I'm sure they did it in private. But all I ever heard was their bitching about baseball.

For what seemed like hours they'd pitch complaints back and forth, bemoaning the weakness of our bullpen, our terrible production in the middle of the lineup, or our general manager's latest mind-bogglingly stupid signing decision. Granted, they had a lot to complain about over the years—the Giants missed the playoffs for the first decade of their friendship, and in 1985 the team lost a hundred games, the most in franchise history. Even when things were going well—when the Giants were on a win streak, or won their division in '97, or somehow managed to sign Barry Bonds as a free agent, success always came with an asterisk. I don't think Saul and Dad complained because they really believed the Giants would never win. I think they held back because, like many Jews, they knew excitement is dangerous; the more you invest, the more you're devastated by the letdown. And no matter how many games you win during the season, it's still gonna burn when you lose the last game of the year. The complaining wasn't just about pessimism; it was Dad and Saul doing their part for the Giants—working to distract the Evil Eye.

•

My first word was *ball.*

Supposedly, my first sentence was *I love you,* as my father was pushing me on a swing at the children's playground in Golden Gate Park, but I have to take his word for it.

My first memory is of the sound of smashing porcelain. Of smiling and clapping in my high chair as my babysitter desperately tried to pin our blue kitchen shelf against the wall, watching mugs magically stutter-step to the brink, dawdle for a moment, and then hurtle toward the linoleum, bursting into shards, the creaky wooden frame of our house rocking back and forth like

Mom's arms. I remember that I liked it. I didn't know that while cups were dancing toward the edge of the shelf, cars were also plummeting hundreds of feet from the partially collapsed Bay Bridge into the water, that this was the biggest earthquake in San Francisco since 1906, or that the reason my parents weren't home is that they were in the nosebleed seats at Candlestick Park, waiting for the first Giants World Series game since 1962, sitting directly underneath a concrete overhang that had begun to wobble like a rubber band. After a minute or so, the rumbling ended. My babysitter kept the shelf up the whole time and swept up the broken plates. The Bay Bridge was eventually repaired, funerals held, the game canceled and rescheduled—nature, just like in '62, reminding everyone of the order of things. When play resumed, Dad bribed the ticket-taker twenty bucks not to tear his stub, so he could keep it as a souvenir. But the Oakland A's swept the Giants in four to win the 1989 World Series, and Dad and Saul lamented— finally a real chance, and we'd blown it.

I wasn't quite *born* with a baseball bat in my hand, but it was close. My mom was in the hospital in premature labor for twelve weeks in the heart of the '86 season, mid-June to mid-September, holding my twin brother and me in, until we could be born healthy, while Robbie Thompson and Will Clark were slugging their way to a rare winning season. Next year, the Giants won the National League West for the first time in a decade, and when my brother and I were three, after the Giants had climbed back to the World Series, we begged Dad to buy us burnt-orange souvenir bats from a concession stand at Candlestick. It probably wasn't a good idea to give weapons to toddlers, but I know what happened next was my fault. Even three-year-olds can be dicks.

After the incident, my parents installed Plexiglas over all the low windows in the house. It must have been alarming for them—finding their twin toddlers happily attacking the third-story playroom windows, chucking their toys through the busted frames to the ground below. Mom and Dad were concerned for the safety, of course, of tiny, soft bodies under a hail of jagged shards, crashing down like sheets of ice loosened from a melting glacier. And further distressed by the fact that their demon babies were clearly enjoying the destruction of property—panicked that they were witnessing early signs of defective character, or, alternatively, that their parenting was responsible for planting this wickedness inside us. I remember thinking that shattering the thin, eighty-year-old glass, easy as clearing cobwebs, was fun—like smashing porcelain. Our souvenir bats were confiscated immediately, but my baseball indoctrination would stick.

I blame my dubious playing skills on a combination of the terrible fundamentals my dad taught me and my own defective DNA. I survived the soup strainer longer than I had any right to, much to the annoyance of many coaches, simply because I kept showing up, lacing my cleats, accumulating crappy gold plastic participation trophies. 1994 . . . 1995 . . . 1996 . . . 1997 . . . 1998 . . . I never made an All-Star game. But I did pick up the 1999 San Francisco Little League sportsmanship award, leaning the plaque proudly against the other trophies on my desk.

The little golden army represented a lot of showing up: from tee ball, wandering the bench in grass-stained jeans, chewing the collars of my general-issue San Francisco Sluggers Parks and Rec shirt; to the Junior Giants, sitting cross-legged in the outfield humming "Take Me Out to the Ballgame," twisting the stems of the little white flowers into bracelets, the occasional fly ball sailing over my head, followed by a faint mob frantically yelling my name; to middle school tryouts on the blacktop, ground balls flying across the asphalt like skipping stones, ricocheting off my ankles, nursing the bruises the next morning as I limped toward the posted roster list that I was sure wouldn't include me, then double- and triple-checking it wasn't a mistake, and leaping down the hallway in joyful disbelief; to high school, after two years riding the bench, the night before the first game as a junior, polishing the special red helmet with number nine on the back that Coach Soares gave to that season's starters. Nine had always been my jersey number, and it was fitting—there are nine players in a baseball lineup, and up until then I'd always improved just enough to ascend to the next level as that team's most questionably qualified player. I lasted as the starting left fielder for two games before being demoted for a freshman, until by midseason, I was sixth on the outfield depth chart, practicing my sunflower seed–spitting technique in the dugout.

I ended my playing days as a bench rider, where you have two job options: scorekeeper and shit talker. I am a shit talker. I may not have played much for my final two lame duck baseball seasons, but I contributed significantly to evolving the art of dugout chatter in the Bay Area Conference League Division Five. I take pride in the fact that one game, after deploying my brand of stream-of-consciousness psychological warfare, some Lick-Wilmerding players were so annoyed that they waited for me in the parking lot. It meant I'd made an impact on the game. In my four years on the varsity high school team, including my few starts, I notched a career total of two hits—both singles—an average of half a hit per year. My final baseball game ended quietly, with a pinch-hit groundout in the fourteenth inning, when coach had no other subs left.

Through it all, I don't believe my dad ever missed a single one of my games. Year after year he showed up in the same puffy red down jacket, sitting yards away from the other parents in a folding chair up the right field line, rereading a Patrick O'Brian historical maritime novel as I rode the bench, dove weirdly, struck out, and misplayed grounders. I did have a small handful of glory moments—a successful sacrifice bunt here, a diving catch there—and my dad, my biggest fan, was there for every one of them.

The only difference between a bench warmer and a fan is that a bench warmer has delusions of playing. As Dad tells it, his two favorite people to go to a ballgame with were me, then Saul. Dad and I made a good pair: I handled the shit talking; he did the scorekeeping. At every game we ever went to, Dad kept careful track of the plays on his spiral-bound scorecard, notating every error, groundball, double, and strike. He didn't mind when I heckled—it meant I was paying attention. Nothing annoys him more than a fan who ignores the game.

Once, when I was twelve, on a visit to Grandma Syde, the two of us sat near the railing of the Shea Stadium upper-deck arcade at a Mets game. His irritation flared when the wave began pulsing around the park, and he stayed planted in his seat as arms shot into the air around us. But his mood fully bubbled over when his arch-enemy appeared: the bouncing beach ball. Dad's shoulders tensed every time the symbol of disrespect bobbed near us, and when it finally bounced onto Dad's score sheet, where he was marking a play, he swatted it wildly—over the edge of the balcony. A twelve-year-old in public with a parent doesn't need any extra help feeling embarrassed, but there's another level of mortification when an entire section of Mets fans chants YOU SUCK! at your dad for two innings. Dad just ignored it and focused on what was important—the game.

I may not have shared my father's outrage at beach balls or the wave, but we both agreed that there was something special about this quirky sport, its bizarre rules, the pace, the smell of the grass, its history and mystique. I was sad to accept that I was approaching the end of the line in my baseball career and managed to briefly extend my time in the game when, one summer, I landed a job as a Giants stadium vendor. I figured it was my dream job, combining my love of baseball with my love of shit talking. I'd be the confident, silver-tongued newcomer, booming out *Getcher salty nuts right here!*, tossing the bag in a perfect arcing hook shot two sections over while the crowd cheered, *Where'd they find this guy?*

My first day on the job, a beautiful summer afternoon game, I took the back entrance into the stadium and rode the service eleva-tor down to the basement. I tucked my recycled uniform top—a collared black-and-white shirt with orange trim, a few sizes too big for me—into my jeans, my Centerplate Corporation laminated pass clipped to my belt loop. Down in the basement, my motley cowork-ers gathered around a plastic folding table, scattered with little strips of paper: HOT DOGS, PEANUTS, SUNFLOWER SEEDS, POPCORN, SOFT PRETZELS. We picked in order of seniority. The hot dogs went first. Then the peanuts. By the time I got to choose, there was only one strip of paper left: Cracker Jacks and red ropes.

Since there's no salary for a vendor job—it's entirely commission-based—the reward for picking early is real. And you can't land any-thing worse than Cracker Jacks and red ropes. No average person has known what a Cracker Jack is since 1930, and the only reason vendors still carry them is because they're mentioned in the lyrics of "Take Me Out to the Ballgame." I picked last at my next shift, too, a night game: chocolate malts. Ice cream isn't a hot seller, I soon found out, in San Francisco's frigid evening fog.

I can't, however, blame my products for my failures. I was sim-ply a shitty salesman. When people yelled at me for blocking their view I got nervous—so nervous I'd count the change wrong. And recounting the change meant I was blocking people's view for lon-ger, which meant they yelled at me more, which made me more nervous. People probably wondered, *Where'd they find this guy?* but for all the wrong reasons. I didn't last the whole summer, and finally accepted the one role in baseball I was ever really good at: fan.

I cared more about the Giants winning than any of the teams I ever actually played on. When the Giants lost the 2002 World Series, I was old enough to care—so much so that when they coughed up the game six lead, I broke a window in my room by throwing a die through the thin glass. I didn't intend it as homage to my past work, although this time my dad was strangely proud of the vandalism. My anger validated how much this mattered.

Saul and Dad took it hard. They'd let themselves hope this time. It was the Herculean steroidal height of Barry Bonds's career, and he was at his best in the postseason. The Giants were up three games to two with a lead in the eighth, on the brink of eliminating Anaheim and the Rally Monkey mascot that Dad and Saul hated so passionately. San Francisco even got so close to winning the series that near the end of game six, Fox started playing an inspirational Giants franchise history montage, before the Angels mounted their desperate, last-chance comeback.

Through two decades, the 1989 Series loss, the good teams and near-misses of the nineties, Saul and Dad had discussed, debated, and kvetched about the state of the Giants. But the 2002 loss was a different level of gut-wrenching. This time it was too painful to bitch about. We'd missed Halley's Comet and we wouldn't get another shot for a hundred years.

It took only eight.

It's tough to spot the changes a person goes through in a decade while you're living through it. I went from a high school sophomore to an adult in Los Angeles. Kids left home. The Giants roster turned over, then turned over again. Saul divorced. He and Dad hit retirement age. Grandma, who'd complained that she was dying for ninety-nine years, actually got around to doing it. A shrinking posture, a bad back, a dead arm, miles per hour shaved off a fastball, a rookie becoming a veteran, darkening shades of cynicism—it happened gradually.

Then suddenly the Giants returned to the World Series. Maybe the moment didn't capture the nation's imagination the way the Boston Red Sox' drought-ending 2004 team did, but it was every bit as epic for us. The 2010 Giants' motto was *It's torture*, because they won so many excruciating games. All season every run was clawed for, every victory a new heart attack. For fifteen straight days in September, they swapped first place back and forth with the San Diego Padres, clinching the division title only in the final game of the regular season. They mowed down the Braves, the Phillies, and the Texas Rangers in the playoffs. Then, after three World Series victories, nursing a 3–1 ninth-inning lead, our bearded closer Brian Wilson went into his windup to deliver the potential final strike, and San Franciscans, whether home or in diaspora— me, Saul, Dad, Mom, and millions of others—held our collective breath, our incredulous faces lit up by glowing TV screens, hearts pumping, blood racing around our bodies, doing the wave inside our veins, each of us asking ourselves if we could dare to get our hopes up all over again. The ball smacked into Buster Posey's glove. He leapt for joy. The Bay Area danced in the streets. Dad and Saul shook their heads in wonder. Forty-eight August 13ths since Dad started caring, the Giants had won the final game of the season.

◎

Psychotherapists are not supposed to kill themselves. *Nobody's* supposed to kill themselves—but a therapist especially. One day, a year after the Giants won the World Series, it happened, and could never unhappen.

Dad didn't understand. How could he have missed the clues? How could Saul have hid it from him all these years? Saul's family revealed it only afterward—after he'd swallowed enough pills this time and it was too late to save him—that ten years ago he'd tried the same thing and failed. At that time he'd made a promise—*never again*—said he was so grateful for another chance and begged them to keep it quiet. How could his family have done anything but keep his secret? How inhumane a punishment for a man grappling with deep despair and a troubled marriage to also strip him of his pride? Suicide is one of the greatest professional taboos for a therapist, as you abandon not only friends and family, but also vulnerable clients. It doesn't set a good example.

Why? Dad wondered.

Who knows. He was lonely. He'd gotten injured in a skiing accident and wasn't healing right. His body was breaking down on him. He couldn't cope with the fact that he was getting older. He just didn't feel like showing up anymore.

I've been to two Jewish funerals: my Grandma's and Saul's. Both ceremonies included a tradition in which each mourner takes a turn shoveling dirt onto the casket—a chance to give every loved one a hand in saying good-bye. The ritual took all of ninety seconds at Grandma's burial. There were only seven of us after all, including the hired rabbi who'd never met her and a distant cousin back from jail time in Florida, who spent the whole eulogy on his cell phone. But Saul's shoveling line, snaking through the scattered Berkeley headstones, lasted almost an hour. It made sense that Grandma's line would be shorter, seeing as she'd outlived everyone else who was around during the Depression—but the contrast was more profound than age. All those people from all those parties Saul had been the life of over the years wanted to celebrate with him one last time. Mom and Dad rubbed each other's backs and fought tears. The graveyard didn't smell like death—it smelled like dirt and fresh-cut grass, like a baseball field.

The Evil Eye's been bored with San Francisco ever since. The Giants repeated as champions two years later, in 2012, and somehow did the exact same thing in 2014. After half a century of anguish, the Giants had won three World Series in five years. Despite the flood of rings, none of the wins after 2010 ever felt the same—all the pressure that had built up over those years had been released. But there were still games to play, and my dad is still my dad. During the 2012 playoffs against the Reds, the Giants losing, the TV commentator described the mood at San Francisco's stadium.

"It looks like a morgue here."

Then, to illustrate their point, TBS cut to a single shot. Of my dad, in his puffy red jacket.

After the 2014 title I asked him if he could have possibly

imagined this embarrassment of riches—that we could possibly be so lucky.

"I just wish Saul was here to see this," he said, adjusting his glasses.

The championships didn't matter. Baseball doesn't matter. And yet, it does. Because we agreed it does together. I don't see my parents now as much as I used to. But if I'm in town over the summer, whether the Giants are in first place or last, Dad and I both know where we're going. We'll sit five rows up on the first baseline. I'll bring my old glove from high school, and he'll get a Polish sausage with sauerkraut and mustard that reminds him of the parts of New York he didn't hate. And he'll keep score, and I'll talk some shit.

What Year Is It?

It's hard to tell what year it is in Hyampom.

There's a homemade suspension bridge there, deep in the Coastal Range pines of Trinity County, a hundred miles from the Oregon border, three winding hours from the nearest "city" of Redding, California. You still can't get Internet or phone service, although my aunt Marion says that two miles up the road you might get a signal by a tree with a sign scrawled CELL nailed to it. The bridge itself is a hundred yards long, its twin coiled suspension wires grinning as it dangles its 380 (I counted) slats of graying two-by-tens from identical wooden towers on each side of a bluff above the South Fork of the Trinity River. It looks like a miniature Golden Gate Bridge. My uncle Jack, Marion's husband, designed it with a friend from UC Berkeley while he was holed up in the mountains in 1973. He'd made the mistake of finishing architecture school with Vietnam still burning, lost his student draft exception, and heard his number called. And that summer, while Jack laid low in the mountains, my mom, her sisters, and their friends helped build it from his plans, one board at a time.

Lying on my back, bobbing up and down in the deep swimming hole under the bridge, I can't believe how permanent it looks, silhouetted against the blue sky. How trustworthy. How safe I feel walking over a structure nailed together by a bunch of twenty-somethings more than forty years ago. I can't imagine my friends finding two free weeks to build so much as a Lego set these days.

There's a rock carving of an owl's face near the abandoned chicken coop, next to the house, just across the bridge. Before I came down to the swimming hole, I saw it leaning against the rickety tool shed and remembered Uncle Michael chiseling it during a family reunion. I recalled marking his progress and making suggestions on how to improve the shape of the beak as we traded insights like two old artistic colleagues. So I was taken aback when I saw JULY 1993 carved under the owl's face—definitely a mistake—since that would have made me seven at the time. *Impossible,* I insisted to my parents.

"Yeah, well, I still see myself as the twenty-year-old who built that chicken coop no matter how old I get," my mom replied.

"What year is it?" a voice asks faintly.

I'm lying on my back, bobbing up and down as overhead fluorescent lights race by.

"How many fingers am I holding up?"

Hmmmm . . . I puzzle, a mess of digits advancing out of the fog toward me. *That's a tough one.*

"Two?"

"Good job, buddy. Now, can you tell me what year it is?"

No, I realize. *No, I can't.*

"We have to give him a spinal tap," the doctor declares, jogging alongside my rolling bed. "In case it's meningitis."

That, I consider, *sounds very disturbing.*

"2001!" I recall, suddenly motivated.

I look down at myself to see I'm wearing my navy-and-gold San Francisco Unified School District gym uniform, an IV in my arm, knees scraped and bloody, thighs spotted with fresh bruises. The fog gives way to a searing migraine. My jaw muscles are locked, the sides of my tongue chewed meat, burning as I probe my mouth to find slices of dead skin hanging on the inside of each cheek. The last thing I remember is running The Mile in gym class—the official one that determines whether or not George W. Bush will mail me my coveted fitness certificate, with the sweet gold foil stamp on it. I remember pumping my legs as hard as I could, making my hands sleek and aerodynamic, desperate for the athletic approval of a president my city despises. I don't remember finishing.

Waking up from a seizure feels like emerging slowly from an awful hangover. The difference is your memories of the previous night don't come flooding back. Your mind is just a blank white room, and you're handed one crumb at a time through a crack in the door. So in that way, maybe waking up from a seizure is more like being born. The first time is the scariest. After that it's just annoying. Everyone around you freaks out, but you sleep through all the drama. Out of the mist a faint voice asks you what year it is, and before you can even remember, you think, *Fuck. Not again . . .*

After my second seizure two weeks later, at the Japantown bowling alley, my new neurologist puts me on a medication called Depakote. Depakote, I find out, doubles as both an anticonvulsant and a mood stabilizer prescribed for bipolar disorder and depression. When I learn its second usage, I'm angry, and fight my parents hard. It just doesn't seem right to swallow a handful of mystery pills that can screw with my brain like that. *What's the point of getting cured if I become a zombie in the process?*

"It comes down to what you would rather put up with," Mom says, "the symptoms or the side effects."

Although seizures, in and of themselves, aren't generally dangerous, there are noteworthy exceptions—seizures beget more seizures and "status epilepticus," a dangerous condition in which many episodes follow one another in rapid succession, can be deadly. But for the most part, it's the rest of the sharp and rigid world that wants to drown you, knock your teeth out, cave your skull in when you're going down. I develop a new consciousness, at all times wondering, *What am I near? What would it do to my body if I fell on it/into it right now?* I learn you can't trust coffee table corners, rooftop edges. You can't trust urinals either—massive grinning underbites that would get a good laugh out of leaving me to be discovered unconscious, pants down, molars scattered across the linoleum. Hard things, tall things, and wet things—double-crossing murderers. Bathtubs are my personal nemesis though—hard, wet, and untrustworthy. Porcelain caskets. For a while we crack the door during my baths so my parents can rush in if they hear splashing. Then I switch to showers altogether.

For the first few months on the drugs I have the head of a fat little boy on a frail body, cheeks chipmunked. I want to sleep all the time. On car rides I sit and stare indifferently out the window, never too happy, never too sad, which makes sense—my mood has been stabilized. I swallow the little, blue, diamond-shaped pills every day for two years, and a lot of the fine print on the side of the bottle materializes. But as much as I hate the pills, they work, and I'm able to phase Depakote out in high school. I don't have any seizures for a long time, even telling people about how I used to have "juvenile" epilepsy—a dangerous presumption, my dad tells me—the kind of reckless optimism that attracts the Evil Eye.

"Can you tell me what year it is?" a distant murmur asks as I bob up and down, lying on my back.

Fuck. Fuck. Fuuuuuuuuuuuuuuuuuuuuuuuuck.

When I can lift my head, I see that I'm still in my gym clothes—a pair of Nike shorts and a sweaty white T-shirt.

"George, what year is it?"

"2008?" I reply, recollecting that Barack Obama was elected president.

"Nope."

Man, could it be 2009 already...?

"George, it's 2014. How many fingers am I holding up?" My head is propped up on a pillow, neck craned at enough of an angle to see three men, one whom I recognize and two I don't, a hazmat box on the ambulance wall. Details float back to me slowly . . . leaving my apartment in Los Feliz, the Easton gym, running on the elliptical machine, sweat pouring down my temples. . . .

Seizures are triggered by different traumas for different people. Lack of sleep, dehydration, the stereotypical flashing lights—anything that stresses your body and overheats your brain. It's clear now that one of my triggers, aggravated by dehydration and fatigue, seems to be exercise, specifically long-distance running. My first breakthrough seizure was running The Mile. With this second breakthrough, triggered on the elliptical machine, I consider that a higher power may be screaming: *STOP EXERCISING! I CREATED YOU TO BE SOFT AND SCRAWNY!* But I concede later there may be something more fundamental to my character at work. Running may pop the bubble, but it's anxiety that builds the pressure. The tension's been a part of me for as long as I can remember—a feeling of restlessness, a density of time, a sense that everything must be accomplished before it's too late. The seizures come at those moments when I press too hard, when I can't remind myself to breathe, when I can't lean back and accept life as it comes.

The week following my breakthrough seizure in LA is tough, particularly because my license has been revoked, and unless you happen to live and work along the route, Los Angeles, where it could take three hours to get from the Eastside to the beach, has possibly the lamest bus system in the country. After years of therapeutic road trips and serving as my friend group's DD, I hate the dependency of asking for rides. It's a regression: relegated again to the backseat on family road trips, staring indifferently out the window.

But it *is* funny, I have to admit, looking around the 704 bus in my Rollerblade liners—Skid Row burnouts sleeping in the back row, runaways headed to the Venice Boardwalk, and Mexican mothers with young children on their way to and from school and work shifts. At first I'd been furious at myself, after skating two miles to the bus stop and realizing, searching my shoulder bag, that I'd forgotten my shoes at home, which meant, on top of the indignity of losing my license, I had to walk through the Chewbacca and Spider-Man impersonators and run my errands wearing Styrofoam boots, officially another lunatic at Hollywood and Vine. But the bus really isn't that bad. There are benefits to getting off the road. It's someone else's job to be stressed out about traffic now. And when I can avoid taking cabs and Ubers, I save a lot of money. No more paying for gas, registration, insurance, tune-ups, and parking tickets. But my bus savings are more than balanced out by the cost of the ambulance rides. The fucking ambulance rides.

Let me explain the emotional roller coaster of the ambulance rides...

"Ever heard of a press gang?" my dad, Admiral Nerd, once asked me.

One of our family heirlooms is a small, old glass-bottom pewter tankard—a trophy my grandpa Clem got in the thirties for winning third place at a college track meet.

"Know why the cup's got a glass bottom? Well, from the sixteen hundreds to the mid–eighteen hundreds the British Royal

Navy used 'press gangs' to trick poor guys into joining up. One of the tricks the gangs used was slipping shillings into the tankards of drunks at taverns—if the coin touched their lips, custom said the drunk had accepted the king's wages. So the guy would wake up from his hangover on the deck of a frigate and be stuck at sea until whatever war Britain was fighting ended. Get it? Glass bottoms—to check for shillings!"

That's waking up in an ambulance after a seizure. The EMTs won't drop you off on the corner and let you stumble home. I've asked. One minute you're minding your own business and the next you come to in an ambulance with a four-thousand-dollar bill in your hand. I've paid more for a two-mile ride plus twenty-minute stay at the hospital than it would have cost me to book a super-stretch hot-tub limousine and a suite at the Ritz. But that's what I get for my stubborn refusal to wear a medical bracelet. I keep telling myself I won't have another.

The approaches to treating epilepsy are as varied as the types of cases. Some serious patients have been successfully helped with brain surgery, removing a chunk of the neocortex. Others, with milder cases, swear by the natural route, sticking with homeopathy, acupuncture, and meditation, some even claiming that by tuning into their body they can feel an aura coming and will their body out of a seizure. The aura is the physical premonition before the onset of an episode. It's a feeling of tingling, warmth, anxiety, and pleasure, different for everyone, that can occur between thirty minutes and half a second before losing consciousness. The more seizures someone has, the easier to identify the feeling. I like my auras. It's like I'm falling in place, a warm blanket draped over me, control surrendered, no urge to fight. There's a pharmaceutical cancel button for auras—a little white prophylactic pill called Ativan—placed under the tongue and dissolved so it enters the bloodstream quickly. People disagree on the degree of Ativan's short-notice effectiveness, but it's a proven anticonvulsant, and since anxiety can be a factor in seizures, an epileptic's conviction in their treatment carries a power of its own.

The mainstream approach is still the daily pills, in a hundred different flavors, all doing basically the same thing: taking a rolling pin to your brain. Since the 1850s doctors have been developing effective medicines, starting with bromide, then phenobarbital and phenytoin, and all sorts of modern twists. I've sampled a bunch of the options.

The drugs come with a telephone book of delightful side effects: Keppra might make you aggressive and suicidal. Lamotrigine: blind and suicidal. Dilantin: uncoordinated, your gums swell until your teeth fall out. Some of the more alarming side effects are rare and could take decades to show up, but what I know from personal experience is that the drugs bring with them the fog—a sense that my memory is being scrubbed from my brain, my history robbed from me. When I'm medicated there are times I need to paw around my mind for a state capital, or that guy from that one movie, or the name of an old friend—facts I know that I know, suddenly vanished. But personal prejudice aside, the pills work, and the only time my seizures come back is when I miss doses. As many very real problems as there are with pharmaceuticals, the drugs have saved countless lives and brought victims out of the shadows.

The wide acceptance of epileptics, however, is a recent development.

Harry Laughlin, born in 1880 in Oskaloosa, Iowa, "pioneered" the "science" of eugenics in the United States. America actually jumped into the game two decades before the Nazis. Harry graduated from the First District State Normal School in Kirksville, Missouri, (now Truman State) before earning a doctorate in cellular biology from Princeton and in 1910 became the inaugural director of the new Eugenics Record Office, a two-story stucco-and-brick building in Cold Spring Harbor on Long Island, forty miles outside of Manhattan, where he worked for nearly thirty years.

Harry Laughlin literally wrote the book on eugenics in America. His 1922 opus, the "Model Eugenical Sterilization Law," was a guidebook for weeding shitty people out of the population. As Harry and other eugenicists, loosely inspired by Darwin's theory of evolution, understood, many shitty people may not realize how shitty they are, inadvertently passing shitty traits onto their offspring and over time making society generally shittier. Shitty people, or what the statute called "degenerative human stock," fall into a number of shitty categories. Although Laughlin wasn't able to plant his own racist views into the text of the legislation, his sterilization law mandated the spaying and neutering of the "feeble-minded," the deaf, the blind, the diseased, the physically deformed, addicts, "dependents"—which included not only criminals, but also orphans and the poor—and epileptics, singled out into their own category.

It wasn't a new bias. Epileptics have been treated with suspicion, and occasionally outright oppression, for all of recorded history. Mesopotamians thought epileptics were being inhabited by the moon god and performed exorcisms on them. Hammurabi (the warlord behind the "an eye for an eye" code) listed epilepsy as an excuse to return a slave for a refund. Witchcraft, spells, poisoning—through the centuries, cultures have found alternate explanations for the mysterious affliction. But the constant is our predictable rejection of the unknown. Even at the turn of the twentieth century, when William McKinley's First Lady, Ida, experienced spells, now known as petit mal seizures, at state dinners, the president would hold a napkin in front of her contorted face until they passed, then continue with the conversation as if nothing had happened. The eugenicists had one scientific fact on their side that modern medicine supports: Epilepsy runs in families. The implication for most was simple—hide it.

It was the job of each appointed state eugenicist to root out the undesirables through field studies. This state eugenicist was legally empowered to subpoena and arrest offenders for their crimes against the gene pool, at which point they would be sent to trial by jury and, if convicted, involuntarily sterilized by medication or surgery. By the end of the twenties, more than thirty states had passed compulsory sterilization laws, many of them directly copy-pasted from Harry Laughlin's guidelines. Eventually, more than three thousand sterilizations took place, and while some American eugenicists quietly supported euthanasia, our own sins never approached the magnitude of Hitler's gas chambers.

That's not to excuse Harry Laughlin from the company he kept. In 1936, he received an honorary doctorate from Heidelberg University for his contributions "to the science of race cleansing." He was invited to receive the honor in Germany at the university's 550th anniversary jubilee but instead accepted in a letter, apologizing with deep regret that there wasn't enough time to arrange travel from Cold Springs Harbor. It's possible the invitation did arrive too late for him to make arrangements. But I wonder if Harry didn't go in person because he worried that while standing on that stage in front of his genetically pure colleagues, sweating in his outstandingly normal Normal School robes, heart racing from the thrill of a good Nazi jubilee, right at the moment when Dr. Carl Schneider proudly draped the purple sash over his shoulders and shook his hand, Harry knew he might sense that familiar metallic taste in the sides of his mouth, feel his temples tighten, and then that brief, lucid buoyancy.

Harry had a secret.

"What year is it, Dr. Laughlin?"

A physician at St. Thomas' Hospital might have questioned Harry in 1926, when, at the age of forty-four, he'd had his first grand mal seizure on a trip to London. Harry wrestled with his own epilepsy for the rest of his life, at one point nearly driving his car into the ocean after seizing behind the wheel. Eventually, he couldn't hide the condition from his staff anymore, having suffered episodes in front of the same colleagues who helped him draft their eugenics policies. By 1939, as Europe descended into World War II, American support for eugenics had evaporated and the ERO closed. Four years later, Laughlin was dead from causes unknown. He never had children.

Polly Miller will be seventeen forever. Most of the people who knew my great-aunt personally have been dead for years, and my family's knowledge about her is sparse. Her legacy is based mostly on hearsay, a series of letters between Polly, her brother Clem (my grandfather), her mother (my great-grandmother), and her obituary in the Sarah Lawrence student newspaper.

In 1942 Polly was just another high school junior trying to figure out her future. Coming from a well-off family in Wilmington, Delaware, she went riding, attended church, took weekend trips from her fancy all-girl's boarding school in Connecticut to the Harvard-Yale game, and to New York to see Cary Grant and Ginger Rogers movies at Radio City Music Hall. Hers was a proper world, and appearances were important.

Of course, there's no such thing as a perfect family. It was kept quiet, but Polly would "faint" from time to time. In the forties both Delaware and Connecticut still had Harry Laughlin's compulsory sterilization laws on the books, and to admit what might be happening was not only to complicate the all-important image of family bliss, but also to put Polly's future at risk. And although phenobarbital was available at the time and effective, she was never medicated.

Polly started to think college might be a waste of time and considered skipping it to get a job as a stenographer. Her older brother—my grandpa Clem, a private training for his World War II deployment—made his opinions clear. The idea of Polly taking an unspecialized job, marrying a bond salesman, and settling into Delaware high society didn't just annoy Clem; it made him angry. He saw compassion and intellectual curiosity in his sister and implored her that there was a world beyond Wilmington—beyond afternoon teas, tennis, and keeping a well-appointed house. He recommended she read *The Grapes of Wrath*.

Clem's argument worked and Polly chose Sarah Lawrence, where she got along well with her classmates, helped plan school events, and decided to major in chemistry. Her analytical chem professor, Henry Keppele Miller (no relation), specialized in compound salt formations. But one day, her sophomore spring, everything changed when Polly fell and hit her head on the bathtub.

"She was developing into an excellent chemist," Henry Keppele wrote Polly's mother in his condolence letter. "I feel very deeply our great loss and it will be something I never understand." It was a bitter irony—Polly never received the benefit of drugs she might have gone on to help develop, her promising life cut short, her brother so bereft he couldn't bring himself to talk about her for the rest of his life.

Thirteen years later, in 1958, Polly's big brother was elected to Congress. Clem Miller was an instantly popular legislator, working hard, keeping late hours, meeting with every constituent he could, building coalitions across the aisle, but never abandoning the liberal idealism already clear in his early letters to Polly. In 1962 he had his proudest moment. The black-and-white photograph hangs in my childhood house in San Francisco: Grandpa with John F. Kennedy as the president signs Clem's bill designating Point Reyes, California, a national seashore.

"The Great Man is home!" my mom recalls her dad joking each day when he'd arrive from work, self-aware of the pomp and puffery of Congress. Mom and her sisters loved their father unequivocally.

Then, when Mom was eleven, everything changed again. Grandpa Clem, stumping for reelection, died at the age of forty-five when his small plane crashed on a Northern California mountainside, victim to the same storm that delayed the '62 World Series in San Francisco. Twenty years after the death of his beloved Polly, Clem followed his sister into the wide unknown. Family friend Bill Duddleson showed up at the door of the Millers' Rock Creek Park house to make breakfast and share the heartbreak. Memorial speeches were given at a special convening of Congress, newspapers printed obituaries, there was a burial in Point Reyes, and after the smoke cleared, a deafening silence. Too late to take Clem off the ballot, Mom's dad became the second congressman elected posthumously. My grandma remarried. The sisters grew up and scattered. And a decade after their dad died, they built a bridge together.

The odds of having a seizure are pretty low at any given time. But floating alone at the swimming hole, it does cross my mind. It's always in the background. No one would hear me. Mom and Dad and Aunt Marion wouldn't figure it out for hours. I'd just taste copper in the back of my mouth, enjoy that warm weightlessness, soak up one fading view of the summer of 1973 graying, creaking, enduring, and no one would ever ask me what year it is again. It's a self-indulgent thought, but it builds a bridge to my parents in my mind. Their jokes about aging and AARP memberships are getting a little more morbid and a little less funny. The truth that anyone can die at any moment, including me, including right now, reminds me that everything is connected, that I'm just a bit player in a beautiful, sprawling epic, and makes me feel as though our conversation up at the house wasn't just between parents and son but old colleagues.

"What age do you see yourself as, Dad?" I'd asked him, next to the stone owl.

"Aaaahhh . . . the continuity theory of personal identity . . ."

"Jesus Christ." I immediately regret asking.

"I'd have to say in my early thirties." He pauses. "You know, maybe it sounds silly but I still feel like I have these endless possibilities in front of me."

"It doesn't sound silly to me," I tell him.

Two weeks from now the worst forest fires in decades will rage across the Trinity Alps, turning acres of century-old pines to spent matchsticks. Marion and Jack will stay in the cabin to clear brush and see their old place for maybe the last time. Everyone in the family will cry and wring their hands and wonder how we'll cross the river next summer with the bridge turned to cinder—or if we'll be back at all. But then the fifty-foot flames will peter out just at the base of the hill and retreat. And by some lucky whim of nature, the house in Hyampom will stand to see another summer.

But for now, my toes peek from the cool water as I catch a flicker of green out of the corner of my eye. I flip over and see a floating grasshopper the size of a Pez dispenser kicking violently, and remember hearing something in a science class I dozed through years ago, about the scales on wet insect wings being fatally ruined, or something. But I splash over to the bank anyway and grab a sheet of loose shale. I coax the grasshopper out of the water, onto the rock, and ferry him to the bank, where he sways back and forth as we study each other, the sun drying my shoulders. It's an incredible creature: beady red pinhead eyeballs popping against his body's fluorescent green, six wiry legs bent crisply at the knee, folded against leaves that aren't leaves at all, but somehow his wings—evolution showing off again. If he lives to old age, he'll be dead in six months. Saving him didn't mean much, but he springs toward me, then hops away, a couple more things to see.

I catch my reflection in the water, pieces of me plagiarized from the past—Dad's nose, Mom's chin, her dad's hair, his sister's brain—and look up to admire the scenery, while I can.

The Boy Who Cried MILF

Sefina

Yo, what do you mean she *ate* her couch?!" Marcus asked, rolling a cigarette from a pile of loose American Spirit tobacco.

"She like, started picking off stuffing from a rip in the armrest," I explained. "She got a taste for the foam and would, umm, snack on little clumps of it . . . like popcorn."

I'd been watching a show called *My Strange Addiction* on the misleadingly named The Learning Channel. And as Marcus and I sat drinking on the outdoor patio at Zeitgeist, a bar in San Francisco's lower Mission, I recalled the segment that had been stuck in my head, of the anxious woman whose only comfort was to eat her seat.

"She hit rock bottom"—I paused to sip my beer—"the day she finished the last cushion. No lie."

I imagined her perched gingerly on the steel skeleton of her beloved couch, one final tuft of cushion in her trembling fingers, a tear welling in the corner of her eye as she prepared to say good-bye to her only friend and step out into the void. Yeah, her fixation was weird, but she wasn't hurting anybody else. *We're all allowed our vices,* I thought, pushing my dry beer glass toward the graveyard of empties in the middle of the table, watching the tip of Marcus's rollie blush each time he sucked a cloud of tar into his lungs.

Back in fourth grade, when Mr. Gomez explained the cruelty of "yucking someone's yum," he framed it in the context of cafeteria etiquette: It's rude to gag at the Go-Gurt your lunch table neighbor is enjoying, no matter how objectionable you may personally find its slimy texture or the sound it makes squelching from its packaging. It only dawned on my classmates and me years later, when we connected the dots of Mr. Gomez's sexuality, that he'd been teaching us a broader philosophy of lifestyle acceptance. That every human has individual desires and needs, and in undermining another person's right to their own joy, we undermine our own. My sexual preference in fourth grade hovered between Sour Patch Kids and Flamin' Hot Cheetos, but early in high school, around when I declared myself a vegetarian, a hip-hop head, a communist, a Buddhist, and a teetotaler, I entered the market for a yum of my own. Older women just made sense.

I've always looked young, and by the time the rest of my friends had hit puberty, my self-esteem was suffering. *This is the year the beard will materialize,* I kept telling myself. As I marched into my twenties and the follicles refused to open, I tried visualizing the perfect handlebar mustache, or chin curtain, pushing the hairs out by sheer willpower. Every six months I'd successfully grow one new, long, pube-like loner, which would suggest to me that although I couldn't see my beard yet, it was there, bunkered down beneath my skin, waiting for the right moment to greet the outside world, occasionally sending a stray up as a periscope to check on conditions, each time deciding *not yet*.

I know what Freud would think about my attraction to older women. I don't care what psychology literature might imply: I love, but am not *in love with*, my mother. *But zhat's exzaaactly what someone in love wiss zheir mozher woooooould szay!* I picture Zombie Freud moaning, lurching toward me, scribbling in a notepad, before I drive his fountain pen into his temple.

A fetish doesn't develop in a vacuum. It blooms in the fucked-up petri dish of a person's life experience: their joys, fears, familiarities, and weaknesses. People don't eat couches just because they're hungry. And although I'm generally attracted to intelligence and confidence, and like the idea of someone who can kick my ass in Scrabble, I believe the most alluring aspect of the older woman ties into my delayed development, fueling a fantasy that this forty-five-year-old divorcée, or this freshman congresswoman, or this risk management CFO could look at me and see maturity. And every insecurity I ever had about what girls my own age thought of me would melt away, their opinions trumped by someone who knows better.

Marcus started taking me to Zeitgeist in the summer of 2008, when I was twenty-one, back home in San Francisco after my second year at college. Ten years older than me, Marcus was the average age of most Zeitgeist customers, where the vibe in the patio's vast grid of picnic tables was a cross between an open-air high school cafeteria and the steerage section of a transatlantic freighter—a bazaar of bikers and bicyclists, punks, hipsters and queers, septum piercings, hand tattoos, and muttonchops.

Marcus alternated between rolling cigarettes for himself and communal spliffs as the two of us, increasingly drunk and stoned, hatched increasingly dubious get-rich-quick schemes. Earlier that summer we'd crashed the presidential nominating conventions to film a crappy homemade TV pilot about global warming, doing the planet's greenhouse gas layer no favors with our two-thousand-mile road trip. On the drive back from Obama's nomination acceptance in Denver, a hyperventilating Marcus lost his engagement ring in a parking lot, and it took an hour of searching through the Dumpster until we found the ring in a discarded Quiznos bag. Marcus and I got along because, despite our age gap, we had roughly the same amount of our shit together. We were a few beers deep that day when he twitched his head toward a far table.

"Yo, that girl's trying to *beckon* you."

It was true. She was a few tables over—a beautiful, curvaceous, coffee-skinned woman in her midthirties, long black locks falling past her shoulders, a hint of a smile on her lips. One might *flag* a flight attendant, *summon* a confidante, *bid* for a bedpan to be changed. But true *beckoning* is reserved for royalty and film noir femme fatales. The woman's hand curled back gently as if she was fingering the air, her sparkling charcoal eyes locked, unquestionably, on me. No doubt about it. Textbook beckoning.

"Dude, go over there," Marcus hissed.

Stoned and edgy, I stumbled across the patio's obstacle course of knees, table legs, and sockless loafers, Zeitgeist's scowling, pierced, and bearded jury sizing me up from every angle. Finally, I wedged myself into a small opening at her table, where she was sitting with a group of female friends.

"I'm Sefina."

We hit it off instantly. Sefina was Fijian and lived in Oakland. She was progressive and artsy. We seemed to have everything in common as only two thirsty people can. There's danger in eagerness—you expose yourself to rejection. But Sefina and I kindled and built our shared enthusiasm, discussing our favorite performance poets, albums, authors, concerts. We looked each other dead in the eye. And her gaze didn't waver when I felt a couple of fingers brush purposefully across my inner thigh under the table. I did my best not to jolt upright. I couldn't believe it. This was a woman whom, at any age, would be out of my league, and all I'd had to do was sit there like an idiot. I'd hit the cougar jackpot.

But then I started to talk about baseball. And high school. And slowly but surely the embers in her eyes died like a peed-on fire, her excitement replaced by a furrowed brow and resignation. I didn't understand. I tried to resurrect our chemistry by shoehorning Pablo Neruda into the conversation, but it was too late. I may not have been familiar with a beckoning, but I was well acquainted with these roaming pupils—the look of someone who wants to escape the conversation.

"Okay. What's up?"

Sefina squirmed uncomfortably.

"It's nothing. Don't worry about it."

I pressed her. What could possibly be so bad? That I liked baseball?

"Okay. Look. When I pulled you over here I thought you were . . ."

What? Older? Cooler? Had more Neruda memorized?

"I thought you were . . ."

What?

She paused. "A trans man."

And there it was. It took a moment for this reversal of fortune to sink in. After the initial numb attack of embarrassment, feeling flooded back to my rapidly sobering body, that warm, fuzzy, floating replaced by queasiness and a headache.

"I thought you . . . you're just not really what I'm into. No offense."

I felt like bolting out the door immediately, but I waited a few beats before getting up, patting Sefina with an awkward side hug, and wading back through the swamp of jeering eyeballs, all aware, surely, of what had just happened.

"So . . . how'd it go, player?" Marcus grinned as I sat back down.

It didn't hit me until later, but there *were* some positives to pull from the experience. It was a bar full of old people—we were part of different Zeitgeists. And even so, Sefina *had* been attracted to me—something about my bone structure was working for people. *So what if it took her thirty minutes of conversation to figure out that I'm a biological male? Why chain my self-esteem to the gender binary? Sefina has a right to her yum, whatever it may be. Whether or not I'm it. I'll find the person looking for me. After all,* I reassured myself, *everybody is somebody's fetish.*

Arianna

Professor Arianna McGill made no secret of her heartache, salting her passionate lectures with occasional bleak acknowledgments of past flames and her bachelorette status. I'd signed up for her intro philosophy class in my last months of college to fulfill a final graduation requirement, looking for an easy pass. But it was the only class the adjunct professor taught, so even though the room was filled with bored seniors, she poured herself into the curriculum, her joy radiating through the minutiae of every lecture. In Arianna's mouth, the mystifying philosophical gibberish that makes a normal person reach for a horse tranquilizer sounded how Neruda sounds to someone who likes Neruda.

She never volunteered her age. If I had to guess I'd say she was forty-four, although I added her on Facebook after graduation and her profile lists her birth year as 1918, placing her at ninety-one years old—well beyond the range of my modest fetish. She had a lovely, unassuming beauty—dirty blond hair in a messy bun, a JC Penney wardrobe of high-waisted jeans and sweaters of all varieties: knit wool pullovers, patterned weaves, the occasional turtleneck.

Arianna stood in sharp contrast to a typical college kid, whose top priorities were figuring out the keg rental policies of Allston liquor stores and navigating their tangled web of friend-group hookups. She didn't spend her time memorizing past sorority presidents; she spent it contemplating life's tragic mysteries. I imagined her alone in a creaky Cambridge attic apartment, pulling from a bottle of scotch, jotting tomorrow's lecture down with a feather quill, snow raking her window. *Why,* she'd muse, *were we given minds strong enough to ask the questions, but too weak to find the answers?! Why are we given so much joy, and splendor, and beauty only to have it cruelly snatched away?!*

I fantasized hanging back after class and coming clean about my feelings.

Look, Professor McGill—

Please, George, call me Arianna.

Arianna—I'm not going to lie. I'm attracted to you. Maybe this is wrong, but as they say, "By a lie a man annihilates his dignity as a man."

—Immanuel Kant . . . you did the extra-credit reading . . . but this is wrong . . .

No! Arianna, "what is done for love occurs beyond good and evil."

Nietzsche! But . . . but . . . that's on next month's syllabus . . .

She'd pull me into a deep kiss and unbutton her cardigan, lock the classroom door from the inside, and a censor blur would wash over our bodies.

The weeks ticked by and I failed to muster the courage to make my move. *After the next class,* I thought to myself each day. *Then I'll go for it.*

"Custom, according to Hume," Arianna explained one class,

"is the manner in which a person convinces themselves that the future will be like the past."

Seats aren't generally assigned in college seminars, but students tend to fall into a rhythm. It was a small classroom, no more than fifty theater-style seats. Each day I sat three rows from the front, slightly to the left of center. And every single day, Bill Riccardi, a quiet guy who always wore the same Ron Paul trucker hat, sat four rows in back of me. I didn't know much about him, other than his trademark hat, the straight black hair that spilled out underneath it, and that he had a job working concessions at the movie theater near campus. But halfway through the semester, Bill landed at the center of an explosive rumor about a dirty video circulating online. Suddenly everyone was talking about it. If you heard a whispered "autofellatio," "to completion," or "I thought you had to get a rib removed for that," in the hallway, you could be pretty sure Bill was involved. The rumor had legs. You could watch the video after all, and if you did—no judgment—there Bill was on the screen, the same guy who sat four rows behind me, on his back, a Ron Paul bumper sticker slapped on his dorm room bed frame, displaying jaw-dropping length, girth, flexibility, and gag-reflex suppression.

Make no mistake—I support a person's freedom to orally pleasure themself in the privacy of a dorm room. And I'm sure Ron Paul would agree that we have a right to our yums. I also support a person's right to share that private moment with the entire world, should they so choose—perhaps our Founding Fathers had homemade autofellatio porn in mind when they enshrined free speech in our constitution—but I admit, an envious thought crossed my mind one class: *Maybe Arianna saw the video.* Why wouldn't she have seen it? We all saw it. And if she *had* seen it—and been impressed by it (and how could anyone not be? The athleticism alone . . .), then why *wouldn't* she take an extracurricular interest in Bill?

I decided that Bill and I were in competition for Arianna. Maybe he had the inside track to Professor McGill with his sexual circus tricks, but I vowed to win her over with my mind. For the rest of the semester this amounted to me giving the most long-winded, self-important answers I could muster any time the professor asked us to describe the Allegory of the Cave or the difference between realism and idealism. Unfortunately, my desire to sound smart was in direct conflict with my desire to slack on our reading assignments, and Arianna must have seen straight through my bullshitting. But in a class full of checked-out seniors I was hopping over a very low bar by showing basic interest in the material.

Class got more casual as it wound down. Approaching the final week of the semester in December, Arianna asked us about our New Year's Eve plans and volunteered her own.

"I'll probably watch the ball drop at home, alone, again."

She said it with an unconvincing laugh, her melancholy thinly veiled. I didn't like the way Arianna sounded jealous of her students. I felt it was beneath her. *But maybe this is a plea for help,* I thought. *I have to act before it's too late.* With one class left, I finally summoned a nerve—one, small nerve—enough to send Arianna an email.

"Look, I know this is a bit weird, but would you get a drink with me sometime? —George"

My goal was to hint unsubtly at my intention while leaving some room for deniability if she freaked out. We were a week away from the end of our student-teacher relationship, and I was twenty-two at the time, safely in consenting-adult land. But still, the advance felt taboo. I waited nervously, checking my email every few minutes for hours. A day went by and I resigned myself to failure, dreading the impending disgrace of the final class. And then a bold-type, unread email appeared in my inbox. I paused for a few moments. As long as I didn't read the email, there was still hope. I took a deep breath and clicked.

"Okay. When? —Arianna"

It was the best possible scenario. *The amount of time she'd let pass*—she must have been wrestling with the choice. *The brevity of the response*—she didn't try to undermine my innuendo. *She's into it,* I concluded.

My fingers shook as I crafted a simple response.

"Friday. 8PM. Miracle of Science in Central Square."

A few hours later she replied.

"Okay."

At the time I was living in perpetual darkness in a cluttered South End sublet. The previous tenant had left all her belongings in the room, so I lived small, wedged into the crannies between my crap and hers. Would I really dare to invite Arianna to this crypt, with its extra mattress propped against the bay windows, blocking any ray of light, its floor-to-ceiling CD shelf of nineties alt rock—Stone Temple Pilots, Blur, Soundgarden, Alice in Chains? Maybe. I'd have to probe her music taste. I waited patiently for Friday, and when the afternoon of the date night arrived I shaved off my wispy mustache hairs and lotioned my balls. But at six that evening I got another bold email in my inbox.

"I can't do it. Sorry."

Three weeks later, after one final, awkward philosophy class, I was gone from Boston for good, back in California for New Year's Eve, drunk in the first minutes of 2010, surrounded by a bunch of college kids playing beer pong and shotgunning Bud Light in their parents' garage. As we shouted the countdown I pictured Arianna downing a lonely bottle of scotch in her Cambridge apartment, tear-glazed eyes twinkling as the skyline on the Charles River refracted through the slush beads on her window.

If Sefina was a swing and a miss, Arianna was a foul tip. She may not have wanted me at the end of the night, but she knew what she was getting and she'd had to think about it. And just the morsel of knowledge that she'd seen me as *an option* helped me stand up a little straighter. I took a deep breath and a long pull from my red cup. *A new year, a new beginning.*

It wasn't a fantasy fulfilled, but it was progress.

Grace

I've always felt like "love at first sight" is reserved for people who don't have much to say. Grace, however, never at a loss for words, wanted me from the jump. We met while I was strapping on my Rollerblades. It was spring 2014, my first day back at Hollywood's Easton Gym since I'd collapsed getting off the elliptical machine following fourteen seizure-free years. After my workout, Grace plopped herself down next to me on the concrete tree planter, right in front of the spot on the curb where a month prior I'd been stretchered down Easton's steep, narrow staircase. Grace, fortyish olive-complexioned, slim with dark hair, sidled up to me so my slender wrist grazed against her sleeve of forearm tattoos.

"Nice 'blades. Where you headed?"

It was the first week in a year of revoked driving privileges, I explained, hence the 'blades, and I was strapping in for the long trip home. Grace leaned in, fascinated, but I was cagey. Since my only other experience being seduced by an older woman had ended in humiliation, I spent our brief chat searching for the catch. I was also extra wary of being hit on at the gym. Usually the kind of women who go to the gym are interested in the kind of men who go to the gym, and vice versa. And even though I was technically *going to the gym*, I don't *go to the gym*, the same way we've had *men on the moon*, but there aren't *men on the moon*. Grace didn't come off insane or seem to have any illusions about me, though, and she asked for my phone number as her ride rolled up to the curb.

"We should hang out," she said with a smile, before punching her number into my phone and pulling away.

Why not? I thought. *What's the point of having a yum if you don't actually . . . have it?*

Cleaning up for our Friday date, I buzzed my chin stubble,

working my way gingerly around my stitches. I'd finally willed my meager beard into something resembling a soul patch, when, a few days after collapsing at Easton, I'd woken up from an immediate follow-up seizure, alone at home, bleeding from a deep, inch-long gash across the middle of my chin. The five stitches destroyed a dozen strategically critical follicles forever. It was a devastating blow—like losing Gettysburg, Normandy, or San Juan Hill. But it was an important lesson in self-acceptance, I reminded myself, to embrace the parts of me I can't change.

Grace and I met that night at Alcove, an overpriced and theoretically romantic outdoor restaurant within walking distance of my house in Los Feliz. We placed our orders at the counter, squabbling as each of us insisted on footing the bill, then sat down at a little round cast-iron table in the warm May breeze to share our life CliffsNotes.

Grace went first and cut straight to the trauma: born to young parents in an alcoholic home in Ohio, ran away when she was a teenager, ended up living with an abusive drug dealer in California to stay afloat; got married young like her folks; got addicted; got divorced before she was my age; turned her life around when she got into motorcycling; broke into the film and TV industry as a stuntwoman; then, after a string of scrapes, dislocations, cracked ribs, and fractured collarbones, moved into fight choreography. Now life is perfect.

I exhaled loudly, realizing I'd been holding my breath while she talked.

"Wow."

"Yeah."

I took a sip of my cappuccino, licked the foam off my upper lip, and reciprocated with my own, less dramatic history. As we gathered ourselves, Grace asked if I'd like to keep the night going at an all-night diner off the 101 near Highland. We walked a couple of blocks down to her car, I let myself into the passenger seat of her black Audi, and our conversation continued through the ride, our meal, and as we walked back to her car again from the diner. It was midnight now, and the temperature had dropped since we'd met at Alcove.

"You look cold. Do you want my jacket?" she offered.

"No, thanks," I snapped, trying to control my shivering.

I'd been wondering all night why this woman had such a strong interest in me, and a theory crept into my mind as Grace chauffeured me home. *Could she have been at the gym, on her treadmill, a couple machines over from me when I had the seizure? Had she watched me get stretchered down the steep stairway to the ambulance?*

The way she sat herself down next to me like we'd already met.... The way she knew all the trainers by name.... She was a regular at Easton; every time I'd ever gone to the gym she'd been there.... The more I thought about it, the more it made sense. Grace had been hurt her whole life. I was her yum, and her yum was weakness—a frail project she could nurture back to health.

I had an unappetizing fantasy of Grace in a leather jacket, revving the engine of her Harley while I sat in the attached sidecar in driving goggles, Grace patting me on the head before we screamed into the sunset, my scarf fluttering in the wind behind us.

Grace squeezed my hand as she pulled her Audi up to my house.

"Talk to you soon."

I walked inside, shut my front door behind me and sat down on the big, blue L-shaped living room sofa, feeling lonely. It had taken four years to make progress—to finally get a rain check on my canceled date with Arianna. But something else had come to pass in those intervening four years: four years.

I'd grown older than the women in MILF porn. My friends had started having babies. And somewhere along the line, the taboo had gone vanilla. The problem with choosing a fetish like older women is you either keep moving the goalposts back, or eventually you catch up with them.

Grace texted me when she got home, but I knew I would let things peter out like usual. I leaned back against the massive, comfy couch cushion, sized up my sofa, sighed, and picked a little at the armrest.

Good Hook!

One general law, leading to the advancement
of all organic beings, namely, multiply, vary,
let the strongest live and the weakest die.

—Charles Darwin

N o joke, she's like a nine, blond, crazy body. She said to me,
*We could have A. Really. Good. Time. Togethe*r."

To summarize: This slammin' chick in the back of the plane
was Down. To. Fuck. Forreal.

My airplane seat neighbor eagerly explained his good fortune
to me with an incredulous "come on, you gotta be kidding" eyebrow
raise. In our first thirty seconds of conversation, this stranger had
revealed to me that (1) he was married with (2) an eleven-month-old
baby back home in Vermont, and he (3) had some very promising
infidelity lined up for the next few hours.

"Zach" (I never got his name but he looked a little like Zach
Galafianakis) was stuck with a middle seat despite his best efforts.
"D" just sounded like it shoulda been a window seat, you know? He was a

squat fortysomething with a thick brown beard, crinkles gathering in the corners of his eyes, wearing loose Dickies blue jeans and a plain white T-shirt draped over his gut like a tablecloth. A pair of Oakleys was perched on the bent brim of his black baseball cap, embroidered in white with the word HARPOON above a cartoon trout. He was a charter-fishing captain, he told me, heading home from the season kickoff in Alaska.

"Oh *yeah?*" I eagerly contributed. For the first time in my life I had something to say about fishing. "I was just up on the Russian River with my buddy for the sockeye opener."

"That ain't real fly-fishing," my new friend responded.

"Well," I admitted, "I was just holding the net, anyway."

Zach ignored me completely, the angler angling his shoulders and legs away from me like guys do at the urinal. His body language said it all:

You have nothing to offer me.

The current was stronger than I expected when I dipped my rubber toe into the water. Kwudi and I wore beige rental boots—the kind that run two-thirds of the way up your thigh and tie into your belt loops, instead of the fancier, full-trunk boots that look like astronaut pants with suspenders.

Fishing under Alaska's "midnight sun" feels like wading through an outdoor casino; the fluorescents hum all night as time becomes an abstract concept, chain-smoking grandmas feeding slot machines replaced by men in baseball hats and camo vests flicking lures into the river. It was 2:00 A.M., but the sun still hovered just over the horizon, soaking the sky, bouncing glimmers of light off of Kwudi's reel, the metal shaft of the net in my left hand, and the vodka nip in my right—the two of which were making it very difficult for me to keep my balance as I carefully lowered myself from the steps' metal grating into the rushing water and marched behind Kwudi toward the center of the river. I tested the strength of each rock dubiously, wobbling, cursing myself for bringing my cell phone and notebook, one clumsy step from destruction. I'd lost the cap to my airline vodka—probably stuck in the throat of a salmon downriver by now—so I steadied myself, polished off my drink, and pocketed the bottle, happy to discover that when I turned my net upside down I could use the handle as a walking pole. Kwudi and I splashed toward an open patch of stream, giving the other fishermen, huddled in clusters every twenty yards, as much space as possible.

The sockeye opener is an annual event. People swarm from all over to fish until dawn, starting at the stroke of midnight. Kwudi had fishing experience and had been interested in the salmon run, but it was pure coincidence that we happened to pull into Cooper Landing eight hours before the official start of the season. My cousin Eli, the third person on our backpacking trip, had decided to pass and catch up on sleep back at the campsite. But Kwudi and I figured we'd probably never get a shot at it again, and at 11:30 P.M. we joined the crawl of cars to the riverhead.

"Can you believe it?" I asked. "We came all the way from LA to Alaska to sit in traffic."

I scanned the radio until I found a crackling country station.

Every time we moved up a foot we'd lose the signal, only to pick it up again with the next jolt forward. I sang quietly over the strumming guitar I could hear through the static.

"Everybody. Yeah, yeah."

"George—" Kwudi interjected.

"Kwudi, did you realize that 'Everybody' by the Backstreet Boys fits perfectly on top of every single other pop song? It's crazy."

"Man, I swear to God . . ."

"My bad."

We finished the crawl in silence.

"It's thick at Deliverance," a family of five announced to us on their way back up the trail to the parking lot, each of them carrying a plastic bag, "Best hole on the river. We all caught out in an hour." Each fisherman with a license is allowed three fish, and no one wants to leave until they've hit their quota. After two hours inching along in the car, our minds fuzzy from the bizarre daylight patterns, we were relieved to hear this would be a quick trip.

And so Kwudi unspooled his line, tied on his weight and hook with its purple-and-orange-plumed lure, and flicked it a few feet into the stream, waiting for dinner to bite. We waited. And waited. Kwudi cast and recast his line as I leaned against the wide mesh of my net, its handle wedged between rocks, nothing to offer him but cheap moral support. After half an hour I flipped my net around and leaned on the hilt, watching the current slice through the webbing, hoping one of the more remedial salmons might blunder in of its own accord. But all I caught were a couple of leaves, the river quiet except for its steady stage whisper.

Good Hook!

◎

"I'll give you twenty bucks to switch seats with her," Zach hissed, suddenly friendly, newly aware that I was valuable to him. Zach, I now realized, was both a scumbag and an idiot. When bartering plane seats, a person has three potential assets: bribery, the seat itself, and the power of guilt. Zach's bribe sucked *and* Zach's seat sucked—he was in a middle. His alleged lady-love was also a middle. And, since middle seats are about as valuable as losing lottery tickets with the shiny shit scratched off, Zach was relying on some universal bro code to sway me.

Interesting offer . . . should I switch from my aisle seat to a middle twenty rows back for this six-hour red-eye? Zach may have pictured me agonizing. *Well, I have the chance to help this chill dude score, hopefully relieving him from the stress of married life and fatherhood. . . .*

At this point, it's important for me to explain the seating arrangement in more detail. Zach was in the middle of a three-row block—nine seats total. Directly in front of Zach was another empty middle seat. Zach's left-hand seatmate was an old man in glasses wearing a neck pillow and a fleece jacket, zipped all the way to the top, the corners of his lips pulled down by the weight of decades, not necessarily in a frown, but giving the impression of one. Sitting directly behind the old man was the old man's wife, whom he'd been split up from. To the right of the wife was a middle-aged woman and her young daughter. In front of me was an athletic nineteen-year-old—let's call him The Athlete—in sweats and a pair of huge headphones. And in front of the old man was a gym rat with a shaved head—I'll call him Stone Cold—his broad shoulders covered by a long-sleeved crewneck that read 5TH ANNUAL BLUE ROCK BIG MARLIN TOURNAMENT. Stone Cold was a man with no time for small marlins.

The gears in Zach's brain turned, slowly.

"Hey, I'll give you twenty bucks to switch seats so I can sit next to my girl," Zach leaned up with puppy dog eyes to ask The Athlete. *Very sneaky, Zachary*, I thought. *"My girl," huh?—liberal word choice.* After The Athlete shook his head and laughed quietly, Zach tried the same routine on Stone Cold, with the same disappointing result. Zach's rotten old carrot kept falling off his pole, but he kept tying it back on.

I didn't like the idea of playing accomplice to adultery. I don't believe there is ever a justification for deceiving someone you love. But I also hate the idea of an unfinished crossword puzzle or sudoku problem, and I drew the following diagram as we taxied down the runway and took off from Anchorage:

A B	||	[Stone Cold]	[X]	[Athlete]	||	F G
A B	||	[Old man]	[Zach]	[Me]	||	F G
A B	||	[Old man's wife]	[Mom]	[Daughter]	||	F G

Here's what we know, I thought. *The only seats available are middles. Zach's not gonna be able to split up a mom and her daughter—might as well cross them out. We know The Athlete and Stone Cold aren't going to trade their aisles for a middle now, and neither am I. There's only one possibility . . .*

"Hey," I leaned over and whispered to Zach, his arms crossed in frustration, resting on his doughy chest like a shelf.

"The key is the old man and his wife. If you take the bald guy's seat, and he takes the old woman's seat, the old woman can take your seat, and your girl can sit in the empty seat."

I was proud of myself—it was the perfect solution—Zach gets the girl and gets away from me. I justified the bogus morality of helping Zach by telling myself I was doing a mitzvah for the old couple. *Who knows how many more flights they have left to share together?*

"Yeah. I thought of that, but I heard them talking. They don't want to sit next to each other," Zach explained. "They're married."

◎

After forty minutes without a nibble, Kwudi and I started making our way downriver. In small increments at first, a step at a time in the water. Then in larger chunks, getting out of the river, trekking down the path and wading back in at more promising-looking spots. But we didn't know what a good spot was supposed to look like—*shallow, where the salmon are forced toward the surface? Deep, where they gather in holes? Near the bank? Near the center?* We guessed and failed and guessed again, the river barren of any life but us.

"What about down there?"

A group of anglers were bunched up at the river bend. From our distance we couldn't tell if they were all in one spot, or strung apart across a quarter mile.

"Might as well."

We sopped out of the water and walked the rest of the way down the path until we arrived at the congregation.

Deliverance delivered.

"Fish on!"

Every thirty seconds a line went tight and a flash of silver exploded from the river. Fifteen or twenty men jockeyed for position on a shallow ford, toeing a steep drop in depth, casting into the hole. A gaunt woman in pink vinyl pants danced calmly downstream, fishing with her baby strapped to her chest. I don't think she was wearing her kid as a fashion statement, or for early-development bonding—she just really didn't have a better place to put her infant down. It was either prop her baby against a piece of driftwood on the gravel bar and let a bear snatch it to raise as its own or strap it to her chest. The baby's toes dangled a few inches above the rapids.

"Walk it down! Walk it down!"

Mom pulled back on her rod, not too hard, letting the desperate fish seal its own fate—the harder it struggled, the further it buried the barb into its cheek. The other fishermen limboed under her taut wire as she coaxed the fish downstream and toward the bank, finally out of the water and up onto the gravel bar. The animal gasped in the open air, contorting its rubbery spine. She picked up a small orange, plastic baton and cracked the fish's skull. It went limp instantly and she dangled her prize, spinning slowly on its line, silver scales catching the 2:00 A.M. rays like a disco ball.

"Good hook!"

It was an average catch, about a foot and a half long. But *Good hook!* seemed to be like the high fives NBA players get after every free throw, whether they swish it or air ball; there was a genuine atmosphere of camaraderie, and with the fish plentiful, the veterans weren't protective of their turf. Kwudi and I edged our way toward the sweet spot. I eagerly drummed the handle of my net with my fingers, standing a few paces in back as he cast one line after another, close enough to pretend I was part of the action, far enough away to avoid a hook in my cheek. The minutes ticked by, then the hours.

"Everybody," I sang under my breath. "Yeah, yeah—"

"George!"

"Sorry, I've had that song stuck in my head for months."

I leaned harder and harder against my net, until I stepped absentmindedly onto a rock that wasn't there. The top of my boot dipped below the water and a cold rush of glacier melt poured in. My teeth chattered. My competitive spirit collapsed. In the exhaustion and disorientation of Alaska's eerie perpetual Twilight Zone, I started to lose my grip.

Kwudi, I feel a tickle in my boot. I think I might have caught one.

The FASTEN SEATBELT sign dinged off like a starter pistol. Zach motioned for me to allow him out, standing before he'd remembered to unbuckle, fighting against his strap. Eventually he wriggled free and took off down the aisle with bowlegged determination. And Zach surprised me again by returning a minute later, followed by more or less the type of woman he'd described to me: a slender Malibu Barbie blonde in a tight black sweater and layered highlights—the type of haircut that takes multiple appointments.

"This is you."

Zach directed his catch by waving clumsily to the empty middle seat. She—I'll call her Nicky because she poked her head through the space between the seatbacks like Jack Nicholson in *The Shining*—had the wide eyes of a sockeye salmon; all eyeball, no lid—just round white golf balls popping against her black raccoon eyeliner. They're the eyes of the terrified, the naïve, or the devious. I tried to figure out which category Nicky fell into as she corkscrewed her blond mop through the cushions every few minutes to pick up her thrilling conversation with Zach.

"What are you doing?"

"Hanging out. I'm bored."

Nicky snaked her hand back and pawed around in the general vicinity of Zach's lap. He wiggled his knees and squirmed when she opened her fist to offer him a few Cheez-Its. Unsure what to do with his hands, Zach alternately laid them flat, palms down on his tray table, twiddled his thumbs, and stroked Nicky's backmeat through the seatcrack. I started a Ben Stiller movie as a cover for my eavesdropping and spied on them from under the low brim of my baseball hat.

When the flight attendant came around, Zach ordered a double whiskey ginger with Canadian Club and Nicky got a Bacardi and Diet Coke.

"Did you get one, or two?" she asked Zach, who held up two husky fingers and smirked proudly as they doinked their plastic mini bottles together.

"I'll watch a little bit of the movie, then I'll bother you again," Nicky said, ejecting her head from the seatback.

But when I looked up from the end of my movie it wasn't Zach but rather Stone Cold who had her attention, and he fiddled with the fast-forward on Nicky's screen, aligning their Louis C.K. comedy specials to the same point so they could watch in tandem.

I love nature shows. National Geographic or *Planet Earth*. Where you follow the breeding and hunting habits of animals in the wild. Most of those shows are shamelessly preferential to certain species while vilifying others. You can, by sound alone, easily tell the heroic lions, with their stirring brass buildups, from the majestic eagles and their smooth violin swells, from the nasty ferret who sneaks in to rob the nest accompanied by a bit of minor-key oboe noodling. It's cheesy but comforting. The music tells you exactly who to root for.

I knew Stone Cold's arrival on the scene deserved a motif of its own, but I'd lost my bearing. I didn't know whose side I was supposed to be on, or who had the inside lane. Stone Cold won on location and looks. But Zach had the history, and doesn't good old-fashioned dishonest hard work count for something? After a few minutes, Nicky leaned over and whispered into Stone Cold's ear. Then the two of them stood up together, along with the hairs on my arm.

◎

For fish that seemed to be everywhere, they didn't seem to be anywhere.

"They're camouflaged," Kwudi explained, "dark like the river if you're looking down from above, sparkling—you know, like the sun through the water—if you're looking up at its belly from below."

After six years knowing Kwudi, his patience shouldn't have surprised me. I thought back to his composure earlier that week at the dive bar on the Homer Spit—Alaska's bitter end.

"I'm buying you a drink!" the stumbling drunk had offered him. "Do you know *why* I'm buying you a drink?" the barfly slurred, shaking Kwudi's hand. "Because you're *black!* And that doesn't matter to me."

Kwudi shook the guy's hand and downed the whiskey, then he and Eli left the bar to get some food, and I started drinking with an eighty-year-old man who'd been watching the NBA Finals by himself. Turned out he'd been on the ground in Houston for all the Apollo and Gemini missions in the sixties as a member of the NASA reconnaissance team.

"Oh, *Buzz?*" the old man said to me confidingly.

On the tiny bar TV, Stephen Curry missed a rare free throw, and his teammates leaned in to slap palms with him.

"Funny story," the man continued. "After Neil took his first walk on the moon and Buzz got called to the surface, he wasn't really ready for the walk and he had to pee real bad. After the mission, the team—the team was analyzing the suits, ya know, and thought the liquids pouch'd malfunctioned. But really Buzz—ya know, he didn't wanna lose steps on the moon, so he didn't bother to fix 'er up—he just went ahead and pissed all down the side of his leg. So just think about that and see if it changes your impression, yeah, next time you see the picture of him in the space suit salutin' the flag—Buzz Aldrin—Explorers Club—American hero—had piss sloshin' all around in his boot!"

I smiled recalling the man's story in the frigid Russian River, the glacier water at my feet transforming into the piss of the second man on the moon. I daydreamed about the lunar landing and imagined gravity diminishing, inflating myself with a sense of my duty and honor.

And then it happened fast.

◎

Stone Cold stepped to the side to let Nicky pass. Zach's eyes widened as she headed toward the bathroom, sensing a glimmer of opportunity. He fumbled to stow his tray table and lurched past his tangled headphone cord, over my lap, and down the aisle after her.

Zach and Nicky were gone from their seats for fifteen minutes.

◎

"FISH ON!!!"

Kwudi was ten feet downstream before it registered that he was the one with a fish on the line. I rushed in back of him, net poised anxiously.

"WALK IT DOWN!!!"

Then he backed calmly and silently toward the bank as I trailed behind him. I did my best to look useful, waving the net around a little bit to give the impression of action.

"GOOD HOOK!"

Finally, he dragged the writhing fish up the gravel, into the air, and dropped it in my net as it muscled in vain against its confines. We smiled at each other and high fived. And then we paused.

"I'll do it," I said.

I'd thought about it while we were in the river. The fish was going to die no matter what. I didn't want to go down as the guy who held the net.

"You sure?"

I picked up a flat rock from the bank as Kwudi stepped on the fish's side, lifted the rock above my head and swung, but my arm hitched a little on the way down. I let go of the rock at the last minute, half hammering and half throwing it, as if cruelty could flow like electricity—from my fingers, through the stone to the fish's skull—as if by letting go of the rock at the last minute, I was letting my guilt dissolve into the air. *It'll be the rock that kills the fish, not me.* But the rock wanted no part in the murder and dodged left, missing the brain. I threw the stone a second time and connected. A teaspoon of blood splattered the gravel, but the fish kept fighting. I threw the rock a third time, and the struggling finally slowed, like the salmon was running out of batteries.

I sighed and dropped my weapon. It was finally time to go. But Kwudi gave me a pleading look that made my stomach drop.

"Now that I caught one . . . I mean, I might as well try . . ."

After three hours waiting for our first fish, Kwudi had decided we needed to *catch out*.

◎

What a slut, I couldn't help thinking—of Zach. I didn't ask him what went down in the bathroom. I didn't so much as invite a suggestive eyebrow raise. I figured it was better left to my imagination. But after they came back from the powder room, Zach and Nicky's PDA soared to new heights. He spread his legs a little wider, his anxiousness having turned to self-satisfaction, and every few minutes an arm crept back like a squid tentacle and the happy couple hooked index fingers.

Their love affair faded fast. Stone Cold was helping Nicky with her screen again—she'd somehow accidentally switched her entertainment system's language preference to Arabic, and couldn't locate her LANGUAGE button, since that was now in Arabic, too. But Stone Cold fixed the problem and synced their screens up to the new crappy Kevin Hart movie. They howled together as Kevin worked himself into one wacky slapstick scenario after another, and Nicky knocked back a Bacardi and Coke off Stone Cold's tray table.

◎

Kwudi, injected with a cocktail of testosterone and optimism, splashed back into the river while I took on the important job of babysitting our dead fish. I'd seen other fishermen stringing their salmon out on the bank, floating their haul in the shallows while casting their rods. I assume they did it to keep their catch fresh. Or maybe they wanted to give 'em One Last Ride in the ole river.

I didn't have any tie line, so I let our dead sockeye bob near the surface in the net's webbing, wedging its handle under a rock. Then I noticed the dead salmon's ribcage rising and falling a hair. And I saw its dead salad tong–shaped beak open and close once, and then again, its dead, unblinking eye staring pitifully up at me.

Shit.

Our dead salmon was alive.

I pulled the net out of the river onto the bank and found a thick branch of driftwood between the boulders. I'd failed before because I was timid, and timidity is its own form of cruelty. I said a short apology, took a guess at where the salmon's brain was, and swung the branch down hard.

◎

The smell was unmistakable: betrayal. Nicky prairie-dogged over the seat and smiled at Zach. But her expression was obviously plastic, and as the minutes passed, the tentacle stopped creeping back. Zach battled his fatigue, a sailor on night watch, while Nicky continued to make regular recon missions, her smile flatter, her lips pinched tighter, her pupils darting more suspiciously with each checkup. It was increasingly clear that Nicky wasn't stopping by to flirt with Zach. She was checking to see if he was still conscious.

As Stone Cold's fingers danced across Nicky's screen, Zach tried to stay awake by firing up a solitaire game, picking cards by grabbing the top of Nicky's seatback and mashing the screen with his thumbs. He squeezed the seat hard, neck veins swelling, sausage fingers landing with a thud, his wedding band catching in the reading light the sleeping old man had left on. I doubt Zach kept his ring on out of reverence to his wife. He couldn't remove it if he wanted to. His finger fat had absorbed it into his flesh, locking it in place.

Eventually, Zach couldn't fight anymore. He passed out and slumped forward, his forehead resting against his solitaire screen, and Nicky dropped her act, snuggling into Stone Cold's shoulder and spreading her complimentary red fleece blanket over their laps. My mind raced wildly. *What could possibly be going on under that red blanket?*

I was so excited to stand and spy from a better angle that I forgot to put my tray table up, and spilled orange juice all over my seat. But I ignored the mess and strolled down the row, doing exaggerated calisthenics, letting my gaze drift to Stone Cold's lap.

It wasn't the handjob I'd been hoping for, but there they were, fingers intertwined.

◉

I'd take the feeling of changing out of wet socks over an orgasm most days. My mood had one-eightied by the time I pulled on a dry pair.

It was now real morning, the Kenai River surging by our campsite in wide, brilliant aquamarine. After two rainy days the sun had finally broken through the clouds, although even under a gray sky, the Kenai, owing to its mineral content, still sparkled like polished jade. I suppose I've gotten used to a world where the sun's rays have to battle through a heavy filter of smog, so Alaska, crisp and loud, like an overexposed photo, feels fake to me.

Kwudi appeared from behind the bear locker carrying the gleaming fillets, the color of grapefruit meat, as Eli fired up our double-burner propane camp stove. Our pan was big enough to cook only one piece at a time. The skin still clung to one side as Eli carefully laid a fillet in the hot oil. The meat sizzled, its bright red fading to a dull pink, the edges of the cut curling up slightly. When Eli decided the fish was cooked, he teased a chunk of the flaky pink salmon into his mouth and laugh-moaned with a tone that said, *It's stupid how good this tastes right now.*

Fuuuuuuuck.

I plopped right down in the pool of orange juice I'd spilled while getting up to spy, cursing as the sticky liquid dampened my underwear.

The old man had fallen asleep with his paperback novel open in his hands. His head lolled back, his mouth gaped, the only proof he was alive his occasional, faintly rasping inhalation. His reading lamp, a single bright spotlight in the otherwise dark cabin, shone down on the sleeping couple, heads leaned together, a blond tuft of Nicky's hair frizzed out where Stone Cold's bald skull had blasted her with static electricity.

Eli handed me a plate and I lifted a forkful to my mouth, wondering what kind of music cue a nature show producer would sync under our breakfast. I liked to think something brassy and triumphant that implied perseverance, but I also knew from the guy who rented us the fishing boots that the Russian was stocked artificially each season from a salmon hatchery at the riverhead, significantly undermining the ruggedness of the sockeye opener. So maybe it might have been better matched with a bit of spooky theremin wailing or some evil drums of war. But all I heard was the sound of chewing and swallowing, the river, and the Backstreet Boys song, still throbbing in my head as I ate.

◉

I know I shouldn't have pitied this pervy, selfish father, but I guess I've got a weakness for losers. It was easier to despise Zach when I thought he had the upper hand. I was, however, thoroughly impressed with Nicky, who, on one domestic flight, had presumably managed to join the mile-high club and fallen in love with another, hunkier guy.

Good hook, Nicky.

◉

We wiped the corners of our mouths with our sleeves and crammed our trash into the bear-proof garbage can.

◉

Nicky and Stone Cold exchanged phone numbers right before our wheels hit the tarmac in Atlanta, jolting Zach awake.

George Watsky

◉

Then we returned our fishing gear—our boots, Kwudi's rod, and my net—on our way out of Cooper Landing and headed to catch our flights home from Anchorage.

◉

And no one said a word to one another as we filed off the plane, light jazz piping in through the tinny speakers.

Three Stories

1

My first house was a three-story diaper. The hardwood had gone soft and gray, the loose window frames rattled in the wind, and if I had to name the color cast by our weak overhead lights, I'd go with Resident Evil Yellow. Our design tastes did the house no further favors—we crammed rooms with secondhand mattresses, mismatched lamps, and sagging, plaid thrift-shop couches, springs pummeled by decades of rotating New England asses. Like any Boston house, it was drabbest in the winter, set against brown snow beaches and skeleton trees clawing at the sky. It was our first home, and we did our best to destroy it.

I'd taken a year off after high school, so I was turning twenty-one the first month of my sophomore year of college. According to my school's rules, twenty-one-year-olds couldn't drink in the dorms with minors present, and since my college friends were a year younger than me, I decided to bolt rather than live under a year of tyranny. I was proud of my maturity, but really, I was a pretend adult—doing adult things backward, getting adult things and breaking them, and soon, living with other pretend adults and hating them.

I did none of the work to find the place. At the end of high school I'd started a jazz/hip-hop group with my cousin Eli—a trumpet player—and our clarinetist friend Cameron, anticipating an increasing hunger for jazz clarinet in rap music, and they'd both beat me to Boston to start music school. They moved out of their dorms and lined up a seedy four-bedroom house in Jamaica Plain, managed by modern-day slumlords Superior Boston Management, an inferior company that stood for cheap rent and corresponding quality. All we needed was a fourth roommate, and Eli and Cameron had a good lead. They didn't know much about Seb Starek, but we were a saxophone short of a horn section, and that was enough.

I decorated my third-story penthouse as best I could on a limited budget. I painted the walls a deep wine, found a secondhand IKEA bed frame cheap on Craigslist, and built a desk from four pieces of unfinished two-by-two pine nailed to a sheet of plywood I'd found on the street. From my writing seat I could stare out my window, savor the view of the pale blue house across the street, and muse over my prized possession—a souvenir penholder—centered at the back of the "desk": a pewter Atlas figurine who, instead of lifting the globe, hoisted a silver commemorative pen printed with the HBO Def Poetry Jam logo—a cast gift for poets who appeared on the show. Any time I felt shitty about myself, I could count on a glance at the pen for a boost of ego insulin, always there for me, no matter the season or what horrors were playing out below.

Even for Boston, it was an impressively shitty January. I gave one obligatory wipe of my feet on the straw welcome mat, most of the gray winter sludge on my soles hitching its way in with me. I pushed in the door and nodded to Seb, standing seven hairy feet tall in the living room, furrowing his unibrow, naked except for his polka-dot boxers and the giant baritone saxophone hanging from his neck strap. He nodded back to me shortly without interrupting his scales. I trudged through the layer of old sax reeds, plush doll stuffing, empty nitrous oxide whippet cartridges that jingled as I kicked them, and the wreckage of Seb's discarded clothes. He'd claimed the living room for the winter—the standup speakers of our shared entertainment system were the only ones in the house loud enough, he insisted, for him to hear the metronome's click over his own honking—and every day he'd bustle in from the snow in his heavy winter layers, trade his clothes for a sax, and blow experimental jazz scales for four uninterrupted hours.

I walked, dazed, through the living room toward the inviting smells of the kitchen, where Eli was in the final stages of plating a roasted chicken breast with asiago polenta. He carefully coaxed a stalk of broccolini inward with his fork.

"Another Thomas Keller recipe?"

"Yeah—French Laundry."

Once Eli was satisfied with the plate's symmetry he pointed

his digital camera down, framing out our crusty kitchen, and snapped a picture.

We'd given up on the dishes in the sink months ago. A couple of unwashed bowls had grown to a massive pyramid of slimy china. We all pointed the finger at someone else, agreeing only that Eli wasn't a suspect. Eventually we gave up and turned the sink into our cupboard. If you needed a spoon you fished it from the cesspool, thumbed off the film, ate your cereal, and tossed it back in the swamp for the next roommate.

I pulled a pot and a pan out of the sink, scraped off the grime, and set them on the burners of our crumb-caked stove. Eli ate his asiago polenta at the kitchen table, watching dubiously as I dove into my own culinary adventure—the same one I embarked on every night—penne with red sauce, shredded Cheddar cheese, and a bottle of Sprite. I opened the refrigerator door, was blasted with the cool smell of spoiled vegetables, and wrestled a jar of Ragú from the tightly packed, largely expired fridge. (Two-thirds of the space was occupied by Seb's industrial-size vat of kimchi, so big that he'd had to remove the middle shelf to fit it in. Seb hit Costco on move-in day, to save money by buying groceries in bulk, and had stocked rations for the next decade.)

When spring sprang in Boston the giant centipedes celebrated by crawling out of our foundation and up the walls. I whistled on the walk home from the train because I had half a plate of leftover plantains and beans in the fridge, a sack of weed in my pocket, and no class the next day.

I came home to Seb, sitting in the living room, sawing the heads off a stack of limp teddy bears and pulling out their fluffy entrails. He supported his music school tuition by selling weed he had shipped to him from a connect back home in California, where his supplier sliced open the stomachs of the bears, impregnated them with jars of bud, sewed them back up, and zipped them across the country. Seb sold the contents of the disemboweled animals to school friends and paid his tuition in cash, reasoning it would be harder to follow the money trail that way.

A ripped fragment of the box was addressed to "John Smith."

"There's no return address on the boxes," Seb explained, "so the post office won't know who sent it."

I walked to the kitchen, where Eli and Cameron were cooking, and sat down on the Hookah Room sofa. Originally we envisioned the Hookah Room, a nook separated from the kitchen by a skimpy bead curtain, as an opulent Silk Road kasbah—fine, draping fabrics, delicate embroidery, fancy cylindrical pillows—a place for intellectual parleys and wild orgies. But in execution it was a drafty square room with a gray, metal-framed futon, a poster of Laxmi on the wall, and a side table displaying the thirty-buck single-hose hookah I'd bought from Downtown Convenience.

I didn't buy weed from Seb, wary of muddying our roommate relationship, preferring to purchase from a kid on campus named Devlin. I crumbled a handful of Devlin's bud into the large hookah bowl, even though I knew I burned through more than I would with a pipe. I liked the theatricality of the hookah. I wrapped the bowl with foil, poked it full of holes with a dirty fork from the sink, toasted a coal over the stove, and set it on top of the hookah with a pair of tongs.

"Cam, you wanna smoke?"

Cameron, a skinny-jeans-and-glasses-wearing El Salvadorian BDSM enthusiast, took a long drag from the hose and passed it back to me.

"Yesterday was crazy," he marveled. "I walked Beth to Midway on a leash and dog collar, and we just sat at the bar drinking whiskey."

The only thing that shocked me was the level of commitment. Cameron usually had new girls over once or twice, but his new girlfriend, Beth, a forty-three-year-old widow, was now commuting regularly by plane from her executive job in Chicago to weekend humiliation sessions in Boston.

Cameron took another drag from the hookah. "It was awesome."

"Cool, man," I replied distractedly.

The coal on top of the hookah had crumbled to ash, and suddenly I was starving. I opened the fridge and pawed around for my plantains, where I'd hidden them on the right side behind a jug of Tampico. They weren't there. I peered in the cheese drawer, checked the vegetable crisper, and opened the shield to the butter bin. Nothing. Just a jug of Tampico and a huge fucking vat of kimchi.

"Seb!" I yelled across rooms. "Did you eat my beans and plantains?!"

A short pause.

"Oh. Yeah. Maybe. I don't know. I'm sorry. I apologize."

I took a few deep breaths.

"Dude. Dude. Dude."

I attempted to make a passionate and measured case to Seb: That this was objectively a pretty douchebag move. That there was very little vegetarian food in the kitchen. That I forgave him but wanted his word he wouldn't do it again.

"Yeah, yeah, yeah, of course not," he promised dismissively as I left the room.

"Remind me why we invited this guy to be our roommate?" I whispered to Eli and Cameron. "He's toxic."

Cameron mimed some sax playing, and then had a thought.

"That reminds me—Superior Boston is gonna spread some rodent poison in the basement," he informed us. "I was cooking the other day and a mouse poked his nose up through the burner on the stove."

2

Beep-boo-dah-beep-boo-dah, dah dah dah!

Beep-boo-dah-beep-boo-dah, dah dah dah! (a whole step higher)

Beep-boo-dah-beep-boo-dah, dah dah dah! (a little higher)

Beep-boo-dah-beep-boo-dah, dah dah dah! FUCK! (higher still)

Beep-boo-dah-FUCK!!

Every time he made a mistake, he yelled, "fuck!" I couldn't tell the difference between the botched scales and the ones that he nailed, but Seb was apparently being diligent about something as the cascade of squeals and grunts climbed the staircase to my room.

It was midnight and I couldn't sleep. My stomach rumbled. I stared up at my ceiling and realized I'd painted my walls an entirely-too-creepy shade of burgundy.

Follow the breath in through the mouth, counting to ten, I reminded myself.

1. 2. 3. 4. 5. 6. 7. 8. 9. 10. Follow the breath out through the nose, breathing out all tension. Anywhere you notice yourself holding tension, release it. Release the tension in your shoulder blades. Breathe and release the tension in your jaw.

Beep-boo-dah-beep-boo-dah, dah dah dah!

Follow the breath in through the mouth, counting to ten. 1. 2. 3. 4. 5. 6. 7. 8. 9. 10. Contemplate the parts of your body and breathe into them: the hair of the head, the hair of the body, nails, teeth, skin, flesh, sinews, bones, heart, liver, membranes, spleen, lungs, bowels, dung, bile, phlegm, pus, blood, tears—

Beep-boo-dah-beep-boo-dah!

Follow the breath in through the mouth. If you have a negative thought, acknowledge that negative thought and release it through the—

Beep-boo-dah!

Follow the breath in through the mouth, contemplating yourself as a festering body, a few days old. Breathe in again and contemplate yourself as a skeleton held together by tendons, fleshless, smeared with blood. Breathe in again and contemplate yourself as loose bones, crumbling to dust. Follow the breath in through the mouth, counting, 1. 2. 3. 4. **Fuck!**

Gradually I felt my anger at Seb melt away. *We are but so brief for this world. The problems of today will turn to ash tomorrow. Why yoke myself to pettiness when we're but dust in the wind?*

For a few moments I felt serene. My pillow cradled my cheek lovingly and a warm shiver coursed through my body. And then a familiar panic gripped me. My brain fluttered quickly through a flipbook of disconnected images: a pile of bones, centipedes climbing up a wall, a towering tub of kimchi, a mushroom cloud. *I'm going to die,* it occurred to me as the walls closed in around me. *Not in some abstract sense, but truly, with finality, pretty soon.*

I acknowledged that I was extremely stoned. But in that high I felt more clearheaded than ever.

I cannot allow my future sober self to minimize the urgency of this Truth. I must leave Future George a message.

I sprang up from my bed and grabbed a Sharpie sitting on my desk. There was only one non-burgundy wall—a white slope next to my window where the house's slanted roof bit off the top corner of the bedroom. I uncapped the Sharpie and carefully scrawled THE FEAR IS REAL in big block letters.

Good. I took a deep breath. It was written in permanent marker, which meant it was official. I got back into bed and fell asleep.

"Are you fucking serious?"

I stared unblinkingly at Seb the next day, holding the empty pot sticker container, *George* Sharpied on the lid in my trembling hand.

"How could you? I wrote it . . ."

"Yeah, yeah, sorry about that." He shifted his gaze around the floor. "I was really high."

Seb returned to his scales.

Beep-boo-dah-beep-boo-dah, dah dah dah!

"Those were from P.F. Chang's, man."

I shook my head and walked into the kitchen, where Eli and Cameron were mincing garlic.

Things needed to change at Kenton Road. And I decided today I was going to start with the hookah water. You're supposed to swap it out after every session, but a year and a half of neglect had turned the liquid into a marbled black nightmare. I disconnected the hose from the glass hookah base while Eli and Cameron finished their conversation.

"Did you see the ambulances across the street yesterday, outside the blue house?" Cameron asked.

"A woman knifed her husband to death in there. It was in the paper this morning."

"That's the window that looks directly into my bedroom," I murmured.

"Yeah. Weird."

I imagined the headline: JAZZ SAX DRIVES LOCAL WOMAN TO MURDER.

"Is Sophia coming to the party tonight?" Eli moved on quickly.

"Yeah, her and Samson. She's leaving town for a few days tomorrow and I'm taking care of her ball python."

Sophia, Cameron's new girlfriend, was short, cynical, generally good-hearted, blond, blue-eyed, and 100 percent vanilla—the BDSM community's term for the sexually unawakened. Cameron figured with a little time he could enlighten her, and she felt the same way about him.

"It's pretty sweet. It's not even full-grown and it's like three feet long." Cameron said. "Hope it's cool I keep some mice in the freezer."

I unscrewed the porcelain bowl of the hookah carefully and carried it toward the sink. But I lost my grip and had an instantaneous premonition of what was about to happen—the satisfying crunch of glass—as the hookah fell in slow motion, my hands frozen, powerless to halt its march toward the floor. And the moment the hookah base kissed the hardwood, the glass split into petals, not shattering but instead unfolding like a blooming onion, releasing its poison.

Holy shit.

It was chemical warfare. The rancid stench of concentrated tobacco and rot sprinted through every corner of the house. The race was on—between me and Eli, lunging for paper towels and sponges—and the trails of stinkwater—bolting downward into the foundation, scurrying between floorboard cracks like escaping rats. The smell overpowered the kitchen for weeks and never fully went away.

I sopped up what I could before the party.

We'd had a handful of gatherings at the house so far—notably my twenty-first birthday—but there was sharp disagreement over whether they'd sucked or not. Most of the parties had been my college friends—epic keggers, according to my classmates; bro-y and uninspired according to my roommates. Tonight the music school contingent would get their revenge: Seb was throwing a "noise" party.

Noise music is not for the faint of ear. The concert took place directly underneath the kitchen, in our basement rehearsal space/ Cameron's sex dungeon, which, like most New England basements, was the type of dirt bunker where you can pull earthworms straight out of the walls. On the far end of the basement sat the mildewing mountain of Seb's dirty clothes that iced over each winter; he often bought new T-shirts when the old ones were too far gone. Doing laundry was square.

Around 11:00 P.M. I grabbed a forty from the fridge and headed down the rickety flight of stairs. Opposite Mount Fruit of the Loom, a drummer battered my blue Ludwig drum set while Seb, a guitarist, and a bassist stumbled into one another, pawing at their instruments. Admirers scattered around the basement showed appreciation in their own ways—swaying slowly, moshing, jerking their elbows with each cymbal crash. One girl stared mesmerized at a burning candle held in her outstretched palm, while another girl jigged around it, worshipping the flame.

The point of noise, Seb had explained to me, is for talented musicians to disrupt the skills they've spent their life mastering, discarding the chords and melodies westerners have been conditioned to find pleasant. I'd rolled my eyes at first, but I felt my narrow mind expanding the drunker I got, and it began to dawn on me that this was brave, exciting art.

Then the drummer climbed onto my bass drum and started smashing my cymbal into the ceiling.

"Dude! Get off my drums!"

Noise music sucks ass, I concluded, teetering up the basement steps, through the kitchen and by passed-out stragglers, up the stairs to my room, clinging to the banister.

A lump under my covers stirred.

"Who are you? Get the fuck out of my bed."

Samson, a friend of Sophia's I'd briefly met in passing, responded to me in grunts. After failing to persuade him, I grabbed a handful of his shirt and pulled him out from under the covers.

"Bro, where is your chill?"

We went through the motions of a shoving match, but Samson conceded and slunk down the stairs. I woke up the next morning to a piercing headache and the smell of putrid citrus, which, traced to the source, revealed the present Samson had left me before collapsing on my bed: a pile of vomit in my laundry hamper.

3

I unwrapped a Reese's cup on the Orange Line tunnel bench, trying to think up something clever to say to Jessie Logan when she came over that afternoon. Jessie was in Kappa Gamma Chi, the community service sorority, a beautiful, intelligent, motivated, slender brunette—the kind of girl who lived in a Beacon Hill apartment that could have been a Pottery Barn showroom. She'd taken a curious interest in me and displayed a shocking enthusiasm to ride the Orange Line out to Jamaica Plain. I unwrapped my peanut butter cup foil one deliberate corner at a time, stockpiling conversation topics that could help me seem normal.

When I got home, Cameron was crouched in the hallway, pouring a bag of flour onto the floor. His eyes darted up to me, but he kept shaking the bag, laying a powder strip along the door threshold like a baseball diamond's chalk foul line. I caught another white streak in my peripheral vision and looked to my left, where there was already a line of powder in the living room doorway. And standing on my toes, I could see another long, pale strip in the wide dining room entrance. It was powdered doorways as far as the eye could see.

"Sophia's snake escaped," he explained anxiously. "I forgot to put the rock back on the tank after I fed it."

Making sure the rock stayed on top of the grate was the entire job of babysitting the python. Way more important than feeding it. Cameron could have done nothing from the moment Sophia set the aquarium on his bureau to the moment she picked it up and been applauded for his efforts.

"We'll find it before Sophia gets back. We'll follow the tracks in the flour."

By now I figured the python was probably slithering underneath the floorboards and through the walls—like the hookah water, another menace absorbed by our house, the Jabba the Hutt of buildings, devouring its subordinates as it grew ever more powerful and disgusting.

I stepped over the powder barrier into the living room, determined to disguise our ash heap as a living space. I picked up the scattered clothes, stuffed them in a garbage bag, and tossed it into Seb's room. I lit a stick of incense in the kitchen, drained the sink, and finally washed the dishes.

An hour later, Jessie floated over our powdered doorways, glowing, organized, and poised, a silver Kappa owl pendant pinned to her pastel cardigan and a green ribbon in her straight hair, falling in shiny chestnut waterfalls around her well-postured shoulders, no makeup, just a little lip gloss and the undecorated beauty of her smiling cheeks.

We sat at the kitchen table and I launched into some of my preloaded conversation topics, trying to keep my eyes from darting self-consciously around the room. But Jessie didn't look toward the sink or the refrigerator, didn't seem bothered by suspicions of what evils lurked inside, didn't crinkle her nose at the faint hookah water smell. She chatted calmly. And I kept filling up silences until she took charge, leaned in, and shut me up. I tilted my head, we kissed, and I softly bit her bottom lip, tasting her cherry gloss.

I smooched like treading water—a smack of our mouths, a tentative tongue exploration, a nibble of the earlobe, repeating the theme with minor variations, waiting for something else to happen. Jessie, however, wasn't satisfied with the pace. She grabbed my hand and pulled me into the hookah room, where she whipped her shirt off with Seb-like speed, unclasped her bra, and lay back on the gray futon, twinkling brown eyes locked on mine, pink nipples hardening in the chilly grotto. I pulled off my own shirt reluctantly. I hadn't mentally prepared myself for being naked in broad daylight, and we rolled around for a few minutes, our remarkably similar chests glued together, until Jessie sat up and took the reins again.

"Let's go up to your room."

So we did.

My pulse raced as Jessie unbuckled her belt, sat down on my bed, and wriggled out of her jeans. This was the most beautiful girl who had ever, and might ever, grace my dotted white IKEA bedspread. Not a girl but a woman. A woman with expectations of performance. I lay on top of Jessie, pressing my thigh between her legs, kissing the corners of her mouth and her neck, running the back of my nails gently between her breasts, trying to buy time for my AWOL libido, grinding my nervous pelvis into hers, Jessie trying harder than she knew she should have to to coax a hint of life from my crotch.

Beep-boo-dah-beep-boo-dah, Fuck!

Seb was home.

The ghost of our murdered neighbor watched us through our adjacent windows, as Seb's avant-garde saxophone blended with a soundscape of rustling denim and skin, the suctioning of lips, melodramatic panting, the muffled thump of our next-door neighbors' death metal rehearsal, and the lingering smell of spoiled citrus. I leaned over to my laptop on my bedside table and put on the Beatles in desperation, which, mashed up with Seb's off-key scales, produced the perfect horror-movie version of "Norwegian Wood."

I begged my body's blood supply to report below my belt, but it fled instead to my wildly beating heart. Jessie sighed loudly and we peeled apart, staring up at the ceiling. Finally, in the stiffening silence of failure, we both knew exactly what the other one was thinking.

"'The fear,'" she quoted slowly from my wall, "'is real,'" the words souring in her mouth. "What is *that* supposed to mean?"

I'd forgotten the graffiti was there.

"Oh, that, ha! I think someone came in drunk at a party and wrote that. Weird, right?"

"Yeah. Weird."

Jessie put her clothes back on with a little extra urgency, and as soon as she left the room, my erection bloomed instantly.

I lay shirtless in my bed, glum and suddenly horny, tracing the lines of my scrawlings with my gaze, noticing details of my bedroom that I took for granted—my red Pamplona belt pinned to the wall, the wobbly legs of my makeshift desk, and, sitting on that desk, the little pewter Atlas sculpture, brawny arms bent backward under the weight of what should have been my souvenir Def Poetry pen. But all he lifted was the heavy air. My pen was missing...

Why is my pen missing?

When I finally found it on the living room floor, knocking around with the whippet cartridges and dust bunnies, it was ruined. I held the silver ballpoint up and stared at the spot near the base where the HBO logo used to be printed. All you could make out now were some faint smudges of black ink, gnawed off by the crush of boots, or maybe Sophia's python. Seb shuffled his feet as I confronted him in the low tone someone uses when trying not to scream.

"Seb. I am very. Angry. Right now."

"I needed a pen to pack the blunt. It was the only one I could find," he responded sheepishly. "My bad."

Seb wasn't malicious. He *was* a jerk, but there's a difference between being an asshole and being evil, and a lot of our friction came from our difference in style. Whereas I was too square for Seb, I was too sloppy for Eli. I was too weird for Jessie, but too vanilla for Cameron. We were all, however, typical of first roommates, dumb enough to throw ourselves together.

I felt terrible for Seb when he was robbed that April. He couldn't explain why he had all his cash in his backpack at the time, but I could hear the despair in his voice when he wondered how he would cover his remaining tuition. He hadn't sensed anything fishy from the prospective clients at first, he said. They had references. Just a pair of normal, nice-seeming criminals. But then the gun came out and Seb, not a fighter, handed his entire stash and life savings right over. I don't know where he came up with the money to finish school, but somehow, he did. And he kept paying his share of rent, just like always.

We bruised our way to the end of our two-year lease and in late August threw our junky furniture on the curb, tossed out the kimchi jar—which Seb never quite finished—and said our goodbyes to Boston, one another, and our security deposit. Sophia's ball python never laid any tracks in the powdered doorways, but one day before we moved out, Seb found the snake in the basement near Hanes' Peak, dead, vomiting white goo from a poisoned mouse it had choked on.

Despite Sophia and Cameron's inevitable breakup, Cameron somehow convinced her it would be a great idea to move into a certain three-story clapboard house that was just hitting the market, seeing as she was looking for a place with a certain best friend who'd once vomited in a certain laundry hamper.

Word is, a week after Sophia and Samson took over at Kenton Road, the third-story toilet fell clear through the ceiling to the second floor. The place wasn't falling apart by accident; we'd broken that home. We were poison rats, and the house was a gluttonous, fat-belly python, doomed the moment it allowed us in. I was sorry for Sophia, but I felt some satisfaction that, after being so profoundly affected by that dump—the best, worst place I've lived—we got to return the favor.

My Third Eye

Dude, we *have* to eat at that one," I pleaded to my friends Nils and Tej.

There were half a dozen restaurants in the Bangalore airport food court with no wait; Sbarro, McDonald's, Burger King, Quiznos, a combo KFC/Taco Bell, and a South Indian chain restaurant called IDLI.COM sat desolate, their cashiers staring out into the sterile cafeteria, shifting their weight back and forth. And then there was Curry Kitchen. Curry Kitchen had almost the exact same menu options as IDLI.COM: dosas, the crisp South Indian specialty rice crepes, rolled and stuffed with potatoes or vegetables; uthappam, a thicker pancake with onions, tomatoes, and chilies cooked into the batter; and a standard roster of dals, masalas, chutneys, and rice dishes. Unlike its deserted rivals, however, Curry Kitchen was slammed with business, its monstrous line kinking its way to the wall, hugging the panel of windows for yards. Almost everyone in line was Indian—businessmen in suits, Sikh men with gray beards and turbans, Muslim men in white woven skullcaps, women in colorful saris, many of them wearing, above the juncture of their brows, a third eye, the little red dot, or blue dab, or yellow point with another bigger circle painted around it, that signifies a gateway to higher consciousness. All of these awakened souls had chosen Curry Kitchen.

"I'm gonna get some KFC," Nils said.

"Are you *serious?*"

It was obvious to me there was something magical about the food at Curry Kitchen. Restaurants become popular for a reason. How could we pass up the chance at a transcendent cultural experience in favor of some popcorn chicken?

"The people have spoken, guys. Let's wait it out."

And so we did.

One of my greatest annoyances is getting in the back of a long line, only to *stay* at the back of a long line as it works its way forward. If no one gets in line behind you, it means you're in the exact same position you would have been if you hadn't done any waiting at all. You've wasted the most valuable investment there is: your time. At first we figured it was a coincidence that no one else was queuing up behind us. But after half an hour of tedious creeping, our stomachs growing louder and louder, we were still at the very end of the dwindling line. When we got close enough to see the register I noticed something strange—customers weren't paying for their meals with rupees; they were each handing the cashier an identical strip of yellow paper.

An announcement in Hindi crackled over the loudspeakers, then was repeated in English:

"Attention travelers on canceled Jet Airways flight 2738 to Chennai, your new flight will be departing from gate 64B at 14:45."

The remaining customers in front of us huddled in conversation, checked their watches, and peered at the digital departures info screen above us on the wall. Nils, Tej, and I figured it out around the same time—these people had been given meal vouchers to Curry Kitchen because they were on the same canceled flight. They weren't in line because it was good; they were in line because it was free.

And we were sheep.

"Fuck."

"Goddammit, George."

After forty minutes of wasted waiting, we finally bailed on the Curry Kitchen line. And although I'm generally suspicious of businesses with website URLs for names, I can enthusiastically recommend the masala dosa at IDLI.COM.

If crowded is equivalent to popular, then India is the most popular place I've ever been.

On our first day in New Delhi, I watched in awe as cabs swerved around rickshaws, rickshaws swerved past cows, and motorcycles zigzagged in no particular direction, crossing freely over the casual suggestions of traffic lanes, all of them coughing pollution into a sky so heavy I could stare straight into the sun, now reduced to a pale moon. We stopped at a traffic light and a young woman, missing her fingers on one hand, cradling a baby in a fold of her faded sari, rapped on our cab window with her scarred knuckles, gestured to her mouth, then gave up and walked away. She was soon replaced by a disfigured man who limped up on twisted legs, shirtless, severe burns connecting his bottom lip all the way to his belly button in a highway of driftwood-smooth flesh. I rolled down my window to give him a hundred rupees, then, seeing the money emerge from our taxi, two more beggars pressed in behind him.

"I don't like the term *slum tour*," Andy, blond, two months into his Indian semester abroad, explained to me a week later at a Mumbai house party. The crowd of college-educated Indian kids—the type who could afford to travel abroad during the sweltering spring months—drank Kingfishers and passed spliffs as Andy, one of a handful of Westerners at the party, backed me against the wall. Reality Tours, he insisted, were the best way to see the real Mumbai. He'd already been twice.

"You have to do it."

Of course, Andy acknowledged, he could understand why some could find it problematic—paying for guided walks through people's front yards, snapping pictures and then leaving—he'd heard the criticisms—"poverty tourism"—he *got it*.

"But doesn't that beat willful ignorance? Shouldn't we get a real sense of what's going on if we want to do some good?"

Andy punched his number into my phone so we could get in touch to coordinate some reality, then I slipped out to the balcony, gazing out at block after block of unadorned concrete box apartment buildings, just like this one.

"I can't stand Americans," a pretty Indian girl said in perfect, lightly accented English, handing me a joint, making no effort to exclude me from her generalization.

I'd come to India to play a few small club shows at the end of my 2014 tour but had tacked on an extra three weeks of travel down the country's western coast. I'd always wanted to see the subcontinent—the rich history, the food, and the music attracted me. But there was also the undeniable pull of something less tangible—a Western fetishism that India is this mystic place you can visit to return transformed and spiritually awakened, where you can buy a private slice of nirvana like a gift shop souvenir. And although I liked to think that by acknowledging that line of thinking I placed myself outside and above it, it had been a tough year for me. In some ways it had been great—filled with love, the opportunity to travel the world to play music in a way I never thought possible—but I'd also had medical and legal problems of my own making, and the grind had been catching up to me. I was searching, and I would have gladly paid for answers.

Nowhere I visited was this brand of retail serenity more fashionable than in Goa. The small coastal state exploded in popularity as a Western hippy haven after the Beatles explored meditation in Rishikesh in 1968, increasingly commercialized since then as an international vacation destination. After bouncing from New Delhi to Bangalore, Pune, the Taj Mahal in Agra, I said good-bye to Nils and Tej in Mumbai and took the train south with my new girl-friend, Nicola, and her posh friend Oliver, from London. We arrived at what was supposedly the height of January's pre-monsoon tourist season, but by the looks of its deserted resorts, Goa wasn't too popular these days.

"The ruble crashed in autumn, so the Russians aren't here."

Clive, our resort's dreadlocked head cook, once described in a newspaper review as Goa's "hippy-raver-chef poster child," rolled a joint, lit it with a match, then passed it around as we sat on the deck watching the brilliant turquoise lip of the Arabian Sea smack against the empty white sand beach.

"It's been a hard year."

Goa's blight was our blessing. Nicola, Oliver, and I colonized the deck's premium couch for a week, served attentively by the overstaffed resort, reading, smoking, and swimming, the beach nearly to ourselves. Clive suggested we might feel freer discarding our clothes. On our fourth day we rented scooters and explored the back roads of Morjim, narrowly avoiding the roving cows grazing by the road. There are no gas stations that deep in the countryside, and we bought fuel from one of the many roadside snack stores that sell urine-colored petrol by the liter in emptied plastic water bottles. I was having a great time. But it was clear everywhere that, like the rest of India, Goa was comprised of dual realities: one manicured for its vacationers, and one lived by those serving them.

"Excuse me, are you Freddy?" Nicola asked as we trudged after dark into his empty beachside restaurant. Freddy's wife sat in the corner, wearing a sari, minding their toddler, who was engrossed in an episode of SpongeBob SquarePants playing on an old PC laptop.

"Can I help you?" Freddy, in flip-flops, dark-skinned, chubby, and friendly, asked.

"We got your name from Clive, the chef at our resort," Nicola explained in a low voice. "He said you could, maybe, sell us some molly."

After a brief negotiation, Freddy rummaged behind the restaurant counter and returned to hand Nicola a baggie and his business card, decorated with a pair of swimming dolphins, encouraged us to come back if we needed cocaine or anything harder, then returned to his wife and son.

I'd already taken my pills that morning—the little round malaria tablets, the big diamond one to stem off traveler's diarrhea, and my epilepsy meds: a low dosage of the Keppra capsules I was weaning myself off of, plus the generic Indian Dilantin I was switching to (a bottle of which cost me $2.50 in New Delhi, compared to the $150 I paid in the States). I couldn't find any definitive research online about the effects of mixing Ecstasy and seizure meds, but in a rare flash of common sense, I decided to let Nicola and Oliver trip without me.

Whether it's because India truly acts as a spiritual balm, or just an effective placebo, I somehow managed to have fun dancing sober in the same spot on the beach for five straight hours to music I hate.

I'd never heard of "psytrance" before we got to Goa, but it's all they played in each of the many dance clubs lined up endlessly along the beach. For all I could tell, the DJ just looped the same techno bass drum from the moment we got to the rave at 3:00 A.M., throbbing nonstop as a stupefied crowd of Burning Man types and a sprinkling of locals bobbed from side to side. An enthusiastic but incompetent devil-stick dancer twirled his flaming rods, dropping them repeatedly, relighting and spinning them again as his once-supportive circle lost interest. Nicola, Oliver, and I danced until eight in the morning, digging little holes in the sand with our feet.

The beggars, wandering between the clumps of dancers and folding tables manned by locals selling Kit Kat bars, cigarettes, water bottles, and hard-boiled eggs, were a constant presence. Generally the ravers ignored the women carrying babies and little boys offering glow sticks and light-up pieces of plastic crap. But when the sun broke over the horizon, one beggar girl in a tattered sari walked up to a tall, staggeringly drunk German partier. She put her hand to her mouth and he pushed her away, but when she pointed to her mouth again, he smacked her hard across to face.

The little girl barely flinched. She didn't even look angry. She just bounced away like those old screen-saver icons that hit the side of the monitor and change direction.

"Hey, man," I summoned the balls to say to the bigger guy. "No need for that."

He looked at me like I was the one who'd just smacked him. For a moment, as he wavered on his feet and I thought we might have to fight, I looked around for loose objects I could pick up from the beach. But then he wobbled away, muttering, "*no need* for that" under his breath every few seconds until Nicola, Oliver, and I decided that five hours of psytrance raving was enough.

Responding to the German was an act of bare-minimum courage. I wasn't sure how to handle the constant flow of beggars either. I know nothing, except that long after we left the rave, the bass drum would keep pumping, the Arabian Sea would keep slamming against the shore, and the needy would keep coming, one wave after another.

Deciding to identify myself as a communist freshman year of high school, I'd started with the AOL screen name and worked backward—a common revolutionary practice of that era. After a bunch of scrapped handles, I settled on "karlmarxmanship," hoping to associate myself with action, accuracy, and radical political ideologies. For my final freshman-year history paper, I resolved to prove that communism was the ideal model for society, but since most of the big-name players—East Germany, Soviet Union, Cuba, North Korea—weren't compelling tentpoles on which to build my treatise, I picked Kerala, a state at the southwestern tip of India, where the communist party had been in power since 1957. What I learned about the state—low crime, religious tolerance, gender equality, and the highest literacy and life-expectancy rates in India—inspired me. But as the years passed I began to realize that explosive class violence and totalitarian dictators weren't my style of social justice, and I backpedaled from communism. Even so, if I were for some reason to launch AIM today, my screen name would still pop up as "karlmarxmanship," and I never stopped dreaming of visiting Kerala.

So after Nicola and Oliver took off from Goa to get back to work in London, and a few extra days reading on the beach, I said good-bye to Clive in Morjim and headed south on my own.

Everywhere you go in Kerala you find billboards with the iconic Che Guevara portrait at the bottom, concrete walls spray-painted with the hammer-and-sickle logo, long racks of waving red hammer-and-sickle flags, and political posters of Friedrich Engels, Karl Marx, Vladimir Lenin, and Joseph Stalin posed Mount Rushmore style, gazing off into the future. Yet a few feet away, another city billboard, a Jim Beam ad, announces:

KENTUCKY ROLLS OUT THE RED CARPET FOR MILA KUNIS.

As I rode from my hotel in a hired rickshaw, it was clear that business works the same in Kerala as everywhere else. Villagers had set up shop along the highway. An old man and woman sat in folding chairs under a big parasol, their blanket showcasing three large melons. Ten yards down, next to a stack of oranges, a younger man waited for customers. Closer to the city we sped past a furniture store with no store—just factory-direct wooden bed frames and chairs displayed under lean-tos made of lashed branches and blue and yellow tarps.

I can't pretend my whole trip was motivated by lofty economic research. Out of the vast state, I chose Kannur in the north as my first stop because I wanted to check out a cricket game, and I knew there was a Ranji Trophy match against Assam only a sunny, thirty-minute rickshaw drive from my hotel. The game was already under way when I walked in the front gate at a quarter to ten, the grass field faded and unwatered. The "stadium" portion of the Thalassery Cricket Stadium consisted of five or six lower boxes, each holding a dozen white plastic chairs, and above it some kind of restricted-access viewing box. There were few enough spectators when I showed up that most of the crowd stopped to look at me, and one man in a V-neck sweater got up from his seat to shake my hand.

"No, no, no ticket necessary," he insisted.

After a few minutes standing and watching, the man tapped me on the shoulder and led me up the steps to the VIP box, for no discernable reason other than the notion that random white guys belong in VIP boxes. There, he introduced me to the president of the Kannur Cricket Association and seated me next to a fat man with a blue-and-red ribbon reading HONORABLE GUEST pinned to his long robe—the kind of ribbon you might award an enormous county fair squash.

Every few minutes an attendant offered a sugar cookie or a small cup of milky tea while, below us on the field, men in white pajamas threw a ball back and forth, ran around, and gave one another restrained high fives when teammates slid to stop balls from leaving the circular barrier. Nobody in the stands cheered, though, and after an hour it occurred to me that I might be feeling the same insufferable boredom I've heard described by people who don't understand baseball. And although the game lasted for three days, the honorable guest left as soon as the milky tea ran out, and I slipped away and back to my deserted hotel behind him.

In retrospect, Goa had been swarming with tourists compared to Kannur, and after the better part of a week I still hadn't seen another guest at the Akkara Beach Resort.

"No breakfast today? Are you sure, sir?"

Gadin, the head attendant, a short man with red hair and a starched dress shirt, banged on my heavy oak door. I got out of bed in my underwear to undo the locks.

"I'll be there for dinner," I croaked.

He knocked again three times during the day. Once for lunch, once for dinner, and once for laundry service.

When I arrived at the dining room, a dozen empty tables were immaculately set, each stocked with a bottle of water, and Gadin was standing there smiling, ready to take my order. After serving me, Gadin reassumed his position standing next to the table, hands behind his back, to watch me eat and attend to my every need. I ate one deliberate spoonful at a time, picking at the top layer of the earthy green puree.

"Mung bean," Gadin said, leaning in, nodding almost imperceptibly.

"Very good." I tried to sound convincing.

Gadin relaxed. We didn't speak for the next five minutes. Nothing but the sound of the spoon tip squelching into the top of the mound. Smacking lips, then gulping down the bite. Gadin's feet shifting. The soft crash of the ocean, mixed with the whirring of fans. Gadin asked what I do for a living.

"I'm a musician and a writer."

His eyes lit up.

"You know the Bee Gees?"

"Sure," I said. "'Stayin' Alive.' Good song."

He pulled out his flip phone and started playing "How Deep Is Your Love?" from the weak speakers.

"The Bee Gees are the greatest."

I chewed. The fans spun. There were a lot of fans in the room. Too many fans. Four fans bolted near the ceiling of the wall in back of me, another four on the opposite wall, each one sweeping slowly in haphazard directions. *How much air circulation is required for two people? How could the four dollars charged to my tab for dinner even cover the cost of keeping the fans on?* I started making arbitrary calculations, shoveling one spoonful of mung bean after another into my mouth. *One guest cannot cover the operations budget of this place. It would be better for them if no one were here at all.* I concluded that I wasn't supporting the resort by staying there; I was running it into the ground.

The song ended, Gadin clicked his flip phone shut, and kept right on standing there, smiling.

I needed a massage.

That was the repeated opinion of Rajan, the hotel manager of my next and final stop in India.

He wasn't wrong. It had been three years since my first and last trip to my neighborhood spa in LA, and my neck was stiff after my overnight journey. I'd slept through most of the three-hundred-mile train ride from Kannur, at the northern tip of Kerala, to the comparatively cosmopolitan state capital Trivandrum in the south. Rajan was there to shake my hand when I got to the station, and he walked me to his car a couple of blocks away. His B&B Malaya-man was considerably less creepy than Akkara, but again, I was the only guest.

You're missing the whole point of coming to an Ayurvedic spa if you don't get the Ayurvedic spa treatment, Rajan insisted.

I resisted him for a while. I stayed in town for my first three days, then, at Rajan's suggestion, hired a guide to see the southernmost tip of India. My leader, Danta, took me first to the Kanyakumari Temple, where pilgrims can watch the sun rise and set over the same peninsula, then to a seventeenth-century wooden fort at the western border of Tamil Nadu, where I saw hints of the utopian Kerala I'd fantasized about in high school. In one of the large public dining rooms of the palace, once the heart of the South Indian Travancore Kingdom, the religiously tolerant Dharma Raja fed two thousand poor people for free each day for decades, his progressive, compassionate regime laying the foundation for the highly literate Kerala that followed. But just two rooms over, a glass case displayed antique torture devices from subsequent conquering empires. I was particularly mesmerized by the cage-suit in which traitors were dangled outdoors until they were pecked to death by birds.

With two days left in my trip, Rajan could sense my stamina to resist his sales pitch wearing down.

I wouldn't recommend an Ayurvedic spa treatment to everyone, but if lying on your back for two hours, butt naked except for a tiny strip of cheesecloth over your genitals, while a guy wrenches your limbs behind your back and rubs oil into every crack of your body sounds up your alley, hop a flight to Trivandrum.

A lot of my mental energy during the massage was dedicated to trying to maintain mindfulness and follow my breathing. And part of my concentration was allocated to suppressing an erection. But what took me out of the moment the most was the slow drip of hot oil onto the center of my brow. Apparently a big part of Ayurvedic massage is the awakening of the third eye, achieved by pouring a steady stream of heated oil into the space between your eyebrows. This, I assume, was meant to help me find inner peace but had the opposite effect.

I have a special relationship with that part of my face.

I didn't have terrible acne growing up. I got zits at the corners of my mouth every once in a while, but the only place I ever *really* had breakouts was right there, over and over again, in the patch of skin under my silky blond unibrow hairs. Freshman year of high school, with the stakes of every breakout sky-high, I'd see that ominous reddish lump forming and be patient for a few days. But then came the itchy trigger finger. The temptation to intervene . . . that little voice . . . *Pop it. Put it out of its misery.*

It played out time and time again with the same bloody predictability Marx foresaw of the revolutionary cycle. The deep pinch would fail and I'd try to dig it out with a fingernail. Then came the inevitable scabbing, the peeling of the scab, the desperate attempt to cover the raw skin with Mom's makeup, the new zit bubbling up underneath the concealer. And there I'd be, karlmarxmanship, in the handicapped bathroom next to the library—the only one that locked from the inside—desperately trying to smooth stolen pink foundation over the crags of my mangled skin, dead center in the middle of my face. Then, after I'd done everything I could, I'd slink to history class and wax philosophical on the finer points of class warfare.

With the masseuse pouring oil onto the exact area I spent my youth desperately trying to keep grease off of, the open spigot on my forehead now flowing in reverse, my greatest insecurities rushed into me, threatening to seep out of every pore. I tried to calm my mind, but thoughts pinballed a thousand different directions, from the incessant pounding of a psytrance bass drum, to the beggars of Goa, to the masala dosa at IDLI.COM, down to my exposed legs and the feeling of nakedness in gym class, lying on the massage table, loinclothed and scrawny—somewhat, it crossed my mind for a second, Gandhi-like—until I quickly recalled relaxing under the cobalt parasols of Mumbai's exclusive Breach Candy Club, attendants serving us momos and nimbu panis as the umbrella shadows gradually shifted on the grass, then a monstrous darkness sweeping toward us, the scaffolding clinging to thirty stories of the JK House with its two private swimming pools, gym, and helipad, four hanging terraces, each one jutting out farther than the last, the building threatening to collapse on the slum below, daring anyone to stand in its shadow, and I couldn't ignore the kneading hands of my masseuse and the awareness that he, like Rajan and Gadin and Danta and Curry Kitchen, was out here to make a living, I was here to provide it, and whether or not I found enlightenment in the process was beside the point.

Afterward the masseuse turned the hot water on in the shower—the lower faucet that drains into the big bucket—handed me a packet of herbal shampoo and left without saying much. I stepped into the shower covered in a layer of oil worked too deep in my skin to wash off, scooping scalding water out of the big bucket with the little bucket and pouring it over my head. I checked out of Malayaman and headed west armed with the discomforting awareness that no point on the globe holds the key to my joy, that travel, in and of itself, will not fix me, and that, if I want to achieve any personal growth, I'm better served to embrace that oily spot between my brows and turn my third eye inward.

The White Whale

"Shoooow meee yooour tiiiittaaaays!"

Ludacris boomed from stage in an echoing rumble, like God commanding, "Let there be light!"

Thus spake Luda and lo, it was so—bouncy and pert, happily flashed by a girl to my left in the crowd, sitting on her stoked boyfriend's shoulders. I couldn't believe my fifteen-year-old eyes. There was music that night, too, but my first Fillmore show was more than a concert—it was an *experience*. The showmanship, the pulsing energy, the history dripping from the walls—the tittays. I was an instant convert, and for the rest of high school I studied the Fillmore's concert calendar religiously, worshipping every chance I got.

Founded at the height of the sixties counterculture movement by a young concert promoter named Bill Graham, the original Fillmore lived fast and died young. During the Summer of Love, it hosted everyone who mattered: Jimi Hendrix, the Doors, the Velvet Underground, Creedence Clearwater, Santana, Otis Redding,

Chuck Berry, The Who, Cream, Led Zeppelin, Pink Floyd, Jefferson Airplane. The Grateful Dead held fifty shows there, and Amiri Baraka's play *Dutchman* was performed on the audience floor during a Byrds gig. Bill Graham would host twelve-hour dance marathons and in the morning serve a breakfast buffet for thirteen hundred people. It was hippy mecca—the cradle of the sexual revolution.

I came to know the Fillmore a bit differently. The venue was open at its original location at Geary and Fillmore for only two and a half years, from 1965 to 1968, but when Bill Graham died in a 1991 helicopter crash, his relatives decided to finish his most treasured project: restoring the Fillmore to its original glory. The music scene had changed a lot since the Bill Graham days, but in 1994 the Fillmore was rechristened with a Smashing Pumpkins concert. The room resumed hosting eclectic genres, becoming, between San Francisco's bigger Civic Auditorium and the smaller Slim's, the main club venue for hip-hop acts rolling through town.

My memories of concerts at the Fillmore form a road map through my adolescence: getting kicked out of the Roots for "providing alcohol to a minor" when I used my fake ID to buy beer for my date (who was older than me); Gnarls Barkley and their band dressing up like short-order cooks and passing out hamburgers to the first row; Jamie Cullum leaping off his grand piano; the Coup shouting "5 Million Ways to Kill a CEO"; revealing to my friend Chris in the balcony of a Michael Franti family matinee, as parents corralled a sea of screaming toddlers on the concert floor beneath us, that I'd finally lost my virginity; being moved to tears when, after Jurassic 5 put on the tightest, most entertaining show I'd ever seen, Chali 2na came right out and sat on the lip of the stage, signing every ticket that came his way, including mine.

From the pale pink chandeliers, the red velvet curtains, the wall of iconic, framed gig posters, the big, gold-framed Jerry Garcia portrait, to the hulking and mysterious tour buses docked in the alleyway, it was all magic to me. At shows, head tilted upward at the stars, haloed by the glow of multicolored stage lights, commanding the crowd fearlessly, I wondered what their view looked like.

Every kid who ever flirted with the dream of playing music for a living has a different idea of success: buying a house for Mom, going platinum, or maybe just driving around in a pickup truck with a guitar and a tent. I never pictured myself playing arenas, or in a hotel room full of groupies. I pictured myself onstage at the Fillmore. That was the dream. That was making it.

The path to achieving that goal, however, was a mystery. One thing I did know from all the lines I stood in over the years was that everyone I ever saw play the Fillmore got there the same way: in a tour bus.

◎

When my road manager, Nils, and I saw the White Whale for the first time in early 2013, we knew it was the one. The 1994 Ford E-350 is less than a bus but more than a van—a long, low-rise, short-haul shuttle—the kind used at airports to get you to the rental car facility, or to drive seniors around the block at old folks' homes. Dried white spray-paint nubs clustered around the wheel well and bumper, where touch-ups had been laid on too thick. Inside, nicotine-yellow foam peeked through tears in the gray, coffee-stained upholstery of twenty-five lumpy bucket seats. A row of homemade cup holders was screwed under the upper baggage compartment.

"Real wood," the seller, Eva, a petite hippyish brunette, told us proudly. "My brother-in-law made 'em custom."

Nils and I had driven twenty miles south on the 110 to the A-1 Self Storage parking lot in Torrance, California, to meet Eva and her husband, Tom, for the walk-around, where they played down all the bus's flaws and raved about its brand-new transmission. Eva had invested in sprucing up the bus to finally realize her long-held dream of leading paranormal history tours around California, only to watch her ambitions evaporate. Apparently hauntings dip in recessions.

Business was good for me, though. Nils and I were planning my second real tour after the previous summer's successful string of trial shows, this time moving up to bigger rooms. To my nervous excitement, we were closing the tour out in San Francisco, at the Fillmore.

It had been more than ten years since my Ludacris concert—a decade full of false starts and incremental progress. I'd recorded goofy little songs here and there during high school, but I started to take music more seriously the summer before college, in a series of Sunset District basement sessions with my cousin Eli and his friend Cameron. Eli and I were born a month apart in the fall of 1986 to two daughters of Clem Miller, each of whom married Jews, settled down in San Francisco, sent their kids to jazz camp, and drove them there in Volvo station wagons. We started recording under the name Mystery Funk Quartet, but that summer's collection of jazz hip-hop songs eventually coalesced into a self-released album called *Invisible Inc.* As mortified as I would be to play the music now, I was convinced of our record's quality, and we played live wherever we could—pop-up shows at art galleries and basement parties. Our efforts, however, weren't being rewarded with the eruption of support I anticipated, so I decided to take matters into my own hands.

My dubious history as an entrepreneur started with an attempt to fill the void that Bill Graham left behind. I decided if no promoters at legit venues would book us for opening slots, I'd become the promoter and book myself. With the help of my friend Marcus, I started pricing out private rental fees at San Francisco clubs and soliciting quotes from possible headline acts. After four different headliners sensed my unprofessionalism and backed out, I finally booked a veteran freestyler named MC Supernatural and convinced my friend Tim's dad, an insurance executive, to bankroll the cost of renting Slim's. I crunched the numbers and figured out how many tickets we'd have to move to break even. And even though we somehow managed to sell out the show, I failed to factor in the most important variable in the concert business: alcohol sales. My contract with Slim's included a four-thousand-dollar bar guarantee, and since we'd packed the room with underage kids who'd gotten drunk in their parents' basements before the show, I lost every penny of my loan.

Four thousand dollars at that point in my life represented a bottomless pit of debt, and although it took only a day to officially retire from the concert promoter business, it took another two years to pay Tim's dad back. After a few days of wallowing in self-pity I went back to the drawing board, seeking new opportunities to squander my limited savings on moon shots—guest verses from established rappers, overpriced keyboards, microphones, and mastering engineers—none of which panned out as I'd hoped. I was determined to master the first step of success: failure. For anyone who insists that taking one step forward and two steps backward will never get you anywhere, I protest: *It will if you're walking backward.*

The same self-reliant impulse responsible for my Slim's debacle brought Nils and me to Torrance and the Whale. I've never liked the idea of throwing away money to middlemen. Why rent if you have the capital to buy? The answer to that question—*limit your risk*—although a cornerstone of business philosophy, never resonated with me. No, the Econoline, with its artisan cup holders, wasn't cheap, but considering the years—perhaps decades—of fruitful touring that lay ahead, it was an investment that would quickly pay for itself. It seemed like a no-brainer.

We had a mechanic in Torrance inspect the bus. He didn't find anything wrong but asked us how we planned to use it.

"Well, just so you're aware, it's not really built for hauling weight around the country," he informed us. "More like, trips down the block."

"He's gotta say something like that," I assured Nils after we left. "To cover his ass."

Since the Whale was a junker, there was no knowing its original purpose, how mortally flawed it was, how many lives it had led, or what stories and spirits it held. If Eva ever ran a paranormal activity meter inside the bus, I suspect it would have been like shining a blacklight over a teen boy's bed. No doubt there were "better" buses on the market. Buses with bunks and bathrooms and even showers. Buses that hadn't been scrapped for parts and rebuilt. Buses with documented ownership histories. Buses that were actually buses. But not in our price bracket.

Eva was thrilled when we told her we wanted to close the deal, although underneath her desperation to make the sale was grief at the impending loss. She was selling off the last piece of a dream. I figured Eva and Tom would recover, though. I related to their baseless optimism. They were fellow entrepreneurs, and Eva already had a new scheme.

"Audio porno," she explained. "Porn is so focused on the visual. People driving get horny too, you know. And what about blind people? Who's making porn for blind people?"

"I don't know," I admitted.

Eva was, that's who. In fact she'd already recorded a demo with her husband and she gave us a free sample CD with the keys.

While the band and I rehearsed in a North Hollywood garage, Nils and our friend Zander banged on the bus with hammers in Torrance. We didn't need all twenty-five seats, so they ripped out the last two rows for luggage space, screwing in a piece of plywood as a temporary wall. They sewed up the ripped upholstery and mopped the floors. The cup holders, we decided, would stay. As usual we had it all figured out, except for a critically important detail.

Apparently, driving a three-axle vehicle over six thousand pounds requires a Commercial Class B license in California, which none of us had. The bad ideas flowed. *How long would it take us to get Class B licenses? Do we have any friends with Class B licenses? Could we just cross our fingers and make pouty faces if we get pulled over?* We already knew the answers.

Enter Paul Hamer.

We got Paul's number from a musician friend who'd had him as a bus driver—he was the real deal, we were told. He'd done One Direction tours, Snoop Dogg . . . As our friend sold it, Paul Hamer was the prince of driving guys like Prince. *We can't possibly afford a dude like that,* we thought, but there was no harm in asking. Paul was sitting on his couch in Tennessee when I nervously called him, trying to hide my desperation.

"It's a two-month tour. Weekly rate plus expenses and per diem. We sleep in hotels, two to a room. And we leave Friday."

Miraculously, Paul wasn't booked up during the run . . . but— of course there was a *but*—the gig was below his normal pay . . . *but*—an encouraging second *but*—he was in a fight with his wife and wanted an excuse to get out of the house . . .

Through the phone I could hear the gears in Paul's brain grinding, the fate of our tour hanging in the balance.

". . . what's the equipment?" he asked.

Paul flew into Los Angeles the day before the tour—the same day we needed to load the trailer with merch, amps, and Kush's modified Hammond B-3 organ. That meant to make the schedule work, Nils had to drive the bus twenty terrifying, illegal miles up the 110 from Torrance to Eastside LA, guesstimating the dimensions of the vehicle, praying not to scrape a concrete divider or a Prius in his blind spot. We said a Hail Mary, promising if Nils made the drive safely, we'd never do something so stupid again.

We left Los Angeles March 8. There were thirteen of us on the road: six in our band plus Nils, the other acts—Dumbfoundead and DJ DStrukt—Mike on video, Ellie as photographer, Emily selling merch, and Paul leading the charge. We headed east toward our first show, in Arizona, laughing, playing music at full blast, optimistic and naïve. The bus ran great as the LA suburbs dissolved into the desert. But just a few hours in, I felt a lumpy little itch in my throat when I swallowed. Throat illnesses are a calamity for a vocalist on the road, and the petri dish of a tour bus is one of the worst places to catch one. That first raw swallow was a dark omen, like seeing all the birds fly out of the rainforest at once. But I brushed off the worry quickly—it was time for a long-awaited moment: wowing the first concert line with our new bus.

The Whale's grand unveiling in Tempe didn't have quite the impact I'd envisioned. The Phoenix area got six days of precipitation in 2013 and March 8 was one of them. The good people of Arizona, for all their strengths, don't have much patience for standing outside in the rain, and it was coming down in fat drops when we rolled without fanfare past the thin line at Club Red.

People seemed to like the concert, though, and as Paul shuttled us back to our motel I was content knowing we'd get another shot at glory in the morning.

The general blueprint of a day on tour is a 6:00 A.M. alarm, quick shower, and brush, 7:00 A.M. bus call, six hours on the road, stopping at gas stations for junk food (and occasionally gas), 2:00 P.M. venue load-in to set up and wire the stage, 4:00 P.M. soundcheck, 7:00 P.M. doors, 8:00 P.M. showtime, 11:00 P.M. venue curfew, load-out, back at the hotel by midnight, rinse and repeat. Of course, there are variations depending on the distance to the next show and partying, but it's a demanding schedule.

Because of the nature of our route—basically a counterclock-wise loop around the country, beginning and ending in California—the tour had a deceptively relaxing start. The group was mostly positive about our transport at first—the bus was running well enough, the seats lumpy but comfortable, the weather mild. And since we didn't have shows in New Mexico or New Orleans, and Texas was limited to a small showcase at Austin's South by South-west Festival, we piled up off-days on our way across the South to Florida. But when we ran out of room to drive east, our luck took a downturn.

By Orlando my symptoms were spiraling and the plague had claimed new victims. We were trapped in the confines of the bus, everyone breathing the same infected air hours on end. As soon as a victim thought they'd recovered, the disease completed a lap around the group, the virus had evolved, and they caught its new, more powerful mutation all over again. I was hoarse by Atlanta.

My bug climaxed on a wet Monday night in Greensboro, North Carolina, but I whisper-croaked my way through the show.

We shivered our way up the East Coast. It was a late winter, and the bus didn't have heating, an issue that somehow failed to alarm us when we bought it. But the shows were packed and everybody got along, for the most part. We sold out Irving Plaza in New York and the Paradise in Boston—the biggest shows we'd ever played—and partied through the pestilence.

As more people got sick, folks started to look for places to assign blame. I knew I was patient zero, but there was another scapegoat: fatigue. Because we rotated room pairings, whom you bunked with could make the difference between a good night's sleep and exhaustion, between health and disease. And as much as everyone loved Paul—he was a fluffy mountain of a guy who smiled a lot, laughed a lot, drank a lot, and ate a lot—he also snored a lot, and snored huge. When it came to drawing partners, big Paul was the short straw.

In general, I did my best to assume the same burdens as the rest of the group, but I wasn't falling all over myself to room with Paul. Eventually, however, my turn came, and my fears materialized when I failed to fall asleep before the buzz saw started. After an hour of thrashing to new positions and plugging my ears with Kleenex, I dragged my blankets and pillow into the bathroom, shut the door, and lay on my back, where I learned there's exactly enough room on an average Super 8 bathroom floor for a five-eleven person to fit if you lie diagonally across the tiles, toes under the sink touching the left and far wall, head nestled in the corner near the bathtub.

Ironically, although Paul was the least likely person in our group to fit into one of the tiny motel bathtubs, he was the only one of us who ever used one. During lunch on the Jersey Turnpike Paul took a hard chomp down, felt a malfunction in the back of his mouth, and finished his bite. He groped his molars with his tongue, checked in a bathroom mirror, and confirmed his suspicion—one of his gold crowns had come loose when he was chewing, and he'd accidentally swallowed it.

For the next few days, Paul timed his bowel movements for when we were back at each motel, shitting in the bathtub, then sifting through the mess with a plastic fork stolen from the continental breakfast nook. I admit I didn't think he'd find the crown. I remembered the chaos inside an owl pellet when we dissected them in middle school, and it seemed to me that finding a pinky fingernail's worth of metal, unsure which crap it would even hide in, would take monk-like patience. But Paul was neither a quitter nor squeamish. He'd once had to clean a bus's septic tank by hand after an iconic sixties folk singer had committed the cardinal sin of defiling the tour bus toilet.

"Famous shit still smells like shit," he told us.

Paul defied any doubters and eventually plucked the gold from the sewage, filled the coffee maker with tap water, dropped the crown in, boiled it on the hot plate, popped the crown back in his mouth, and hopped right back behind the wheel.

He may not have been the quietest roommate, but Paul Hamer was a marvelous dude. While everyone else was figuring out how to stay healthy by avoiding him, Paul whistled along obliviously—

vibrant, happy, and, according to him, extremely regular. By Canada everyone had been sick except Paul. But the illness faded into the background, no longer a news story, just an accepted reality of the tour. It was time for the Whale to be the star.

The sun struggled weakly through a chilly blue sky as we followed the same path the St. Lawrence River takes into the mouth of Lake Ontario. Toronto was our second-biggest show of the tour, behind only the Fillmore, so we left plenty of time to make the trip. But somewhere on the road from the border to Toronto, our engine started hiccupping. It wasn't much at first, but the growls from under the hood became increasingly alarming, and we pulled over by the side of the road. Paul couldn't diagnose the problem, and we decided our only chance to make the gig was to let the engine rumble and hope for the best.

By the time we reached the Toronto city limits we were late for soundcheck, moving ten miles an hour with Paul flooring the gas. I held my breath as we slowly approached the venue, cars honking their way around us.

There was already a line down the block when we made it to the Phoenix Concert Theatre. This was what I'd been after—an audience for our bus. But my stomach churned as the Whale lumbered past the early arrivals toward the loading dock, pouring white smoke from under the hood, the engine struggling harder with each pregnant yard. Our water broke just as we pulled in, a big burp of engine fluid splashing the cold sidewalk.

I know it was stupid to be ashamed, but I couldn't help thinking that if I'd been a high schooler in line at the Fillmore, and the

Roots had pulled up late in a sputtering VW camper, it might have made me question the legitimacy of their operation. But even when our bus wasn't combusting, I was finding plenty to be self-conscious about—*a real band wouldn't have* U-HAUL *plastered across their trailer,* I thought. *A real band would have* DOS EQUIS *or* MONSTER ENERGY DRINKS *plastered across* their *trailer.* It was the same misguided flailing that prompted me to ask my parents to drop me off a little ways up the block for dances or concerts when I was younger.

I shook off my insecurities for the moment and headed into the Phoenix, knowing once you get in the doors the only thing that matters is if you put on a good show. Toronto was one of our best—a truly transcendent night. Up on stage it was impossible to stress, but when the show was over, I got right back to it.

How the fuck are we gonna get to tomorrow's show in Buffalo?

God bless Canada. If I could have found him, I would have kissed my old Canadian gym teacher just for being so wonderfully Canadian.

With our rental options crippled by the weekend and the international border, a few of the Toronto venue's Good Samaritan crew members drove us in a caravan of pickup trucks the two hours to Buffalo. It was a beautiful day in upstate New York when we pulled into the venue early the next morning. We waved the Canadian crew good-bye and, while we loaded in, Nils took a cab to Penske and booked a moving truck one-way from Buffalo to

Chicago. After the gig, we chucked our gear in the Penske's cavernous cargo space, and, with no other way to get to the hotel, the band climbed into the back of the moving truck, rolled the metal door down behind us and perched on top of the boxes and amps, sliding around with each unanticipated turn, drinking our leftover greenroom beer, singing and freestyling in the dark. When we pulled past the line in Cleveland the next day in our green Penske truck and two rental sedans, I didn't feel self-conscious. I was proud we'd made it.

After Cleveland was Ann Arbor. Paul, who had stayed behind in Toronto with the Whale, called us that morning with the prognosis: a blown transmission. Since none of the shops were open on the weekend, the best-case scenario was for him to wait at the hotel, try not to go stir crazy, and meet us in Chicago. He could get it fixed and fully warrantied, but the timing was gonna be tight and the repair wouldn't come cheap. My old nemesis—four thousand dollars. I shook my head, my investment now seeming considerably less savvy. Maybe this was Canada with its hand out, back to collect what I owed: tusk-smuggling tax.

Our trucks and rental cars were due back in Chicago before closing hours on Tuesday, which meant if Paul couldn't make it to us at the Bottom Lounge before the end of the show, we'd be stranded with our gear and no backup option. But once again we put our faith in the plan, and when we walked out of the club, there they were, the mighty White Whale and Paul Hamer, gleaming in the moonlight.

Paul didn't tell anyone that he was planning on stage diving the next night in Madison. But during our encore, he climbed onstage and sailed majestically through the Wisconsin air, cannonballing toward the front row in slow motion, his chassis rotating like the bone in *2001: A Space Odyssey*, and somehow, in a moment in which the laws of time and space became irrelevant, a bunch of spindly armed teenagers managed to hold up likely the fattest man to ever crowd surf.

Call Paul Ishmael. From that point on, if I would have woken from a nap to see Paul, Big Gulp in one fist, rack of ribs in the other, no hands on the wheel, steering with his gut, I would have closed my eyes and nodded off again, confident in my captain.

But Paul's noble driving couldn't save the Whale, and as we pushed across the plains, our bus continued its descent into Flintstones car status. Its double saloon-style doors, powered by a feeble gearbox connected to a crank near the driver's seat, had always been sketchy. But when the doors stuck one day in Iowa, Paul took apart the gearbox, then reassembled it. For a few days the crank worked better than ever. But in Kansas, when the doors started acting up again, we resorted to yanking them shut manually, the machinery screaming as we mangled its innards. Finally, some crucial piece of metal snapped and from then on the left door hung limp, refusing to close the last few inches that sealed its rubber edges. The doors' permanent yawn wasn't much of an issue in the warm April weather though, mostly making for a pleasant cross-breeze.

That changed the night of the sixteenth. A freak spring blizzard howled in full force as we climbed into the Rockies in the belly of the Whale. It was a slugging match between two fading heavyweights: The last gasp of winter battering the side of our tired bus. Snowdrifts piled alongside the highway as we inched toward Denver behind a winding mile of glowing red taillights, Paul gripping the wheel tightly. It was the only time I ever saw him sweat, focusing with all his might to keep our trailer from fishtailing off the steep and icy roads. It was a long way down.

Swirls of snowflakes blew into the bus through the gap in our broken doors, sugaring the people in the front two rows. Not just a couple of flakes, but enough to gather in piles. We usually wore hoodies underneath jackets in the bus, but that night we raided luggage for extra layers of clothing and blankets, folding spare T-shirts to use as pillows against the cold glass, half the crew hacking from the third mutation of our plague, the other half leaning as far away from the infected as possible.

Morale was down when we finally made it to our hotel, near Invesco Field, and we left tall footprints in the powder on our way to the lobby. But by the next morning the weather had turned dramatically. Colorado remembered it was springtime and the snow retreated as quickly as it had come.

After the Rockies the Pacific Northwest felt like a victory lap. Our route took us from Salt Lake City to Boise, Idaho, then to Portland and Seattle, punctuated by a quick stab back into Canada to play Vancouver. The weather held, and so did our ride. With Seattle down we had only two shows left: San Francisco and Los

Angeles. But there was a full week gap between SF and LA, so in terms of the grind of the tour, we just had one last push—down the West Coast to San Francisco.

To the Fillmore.

While Eli and I were growing up our houses sat just a mile and a half apart, separated by seven city blocks and Golden Gate Park. On my side of the park was the Richmond District; on his side the Sunset. Both neighborhoods, built on top of San Francisco's one-time sand dunes, each stretching fifty blocks in a grid system out to Ocean Beach, have a lot in common: residential, middle class, heavily Asian. But Richmond kids and Sunset kids tend to focus on our neighborhoods' differences, not similarities. A Richmond kid will forever swear that the Richmond is better, and a Sunset kid will say the opposite. Of course, the Richmond kid is right, but I'd never rub that in a Sunsetter's face.

When my family went over to Eli's house for Thanksgivings, we'd take the family station wagon and park it on the near-vertical hill. But when I was recording music around the corner from Eli's house at Cameron's place, I walked. I made the trip over and over again. From Fifth and Fulton, up the hill into the eucalyptus trees, along the path that separates the chess tables from the meadows where they stage Shakespeare in the Park, through the Conservatory of Flowers, to the left of the tennis courts and the right of the Big Rec baseball diamond, hard left out of the park onto Ninth

Avenue, up four blocks, right on Lawton, left on Twelfth, and two steep blocks uphill toward Twin Peaks.

That's where the White Whale died. She convulsed, went belly-up, and burped out one last gasp of transmission fluid at Twelfth and Lawton—right in front of the ivy-covered flat where Eli's parents still live. The Whale had hauled a seven-thousand-mile loop around North America, and it was the hills of San Francisco that ran the final harpoon through its heart.

We were stranded just a few miles from the Fillmore. No one in our group was particularly concerned that the Whale had died again, though. *Of course it did,* we said with shrugs. After a tour where so much had gone wrong, yet still gone right, it felt fitting. We figured we'd find a way to make it work.

In the moment I'd waited ten years for, I didn't pull up to the Fillmore in a tour bus—not even in a green Penske; I rolled up in my folks' station wagon. The car was so crammed with merch that I rode between my mom and dad, perched on top of the front center console, Eli convoying right behind us in his parents' Volvo. This time, after years of begging to be dropped off on the corner, we drove right up past the line and into the loading dock.

It's a weird thing to fulfill your childhood dream. There's a danger that the moment can never live up to the hype. But the show at the Fillmore was one of the few times in my life when my fantasy and reality synced up.

Once, when I was eleven years old, in Little League, holding on to the chain-link dugout fence of Connie Knudsen Field in Sausalito, I decided I would take the first of several carefully chosen mental pictures I planned to scatter over the rest of my life, absorbing every detail of sight, sound, touch, smell, and feeling I could manage in order to bury a memory time capsule in my brain, to remind myself of the permanence of that moment, the way life felt at eleven—that I will always be that kid—of the smell of cut grass, the snug fit of knee-high baseball socks, a well-curved brim, and my dad in the stands, watching.

I've been stingy with the snapshots since then, so as not to cheapen the first. I've taken only two more—one, lying on my back on a speedboat in India with my girlfriend, passing a joint back and forth, looking up at the flags blowing in the wind as a school of flying fish skimmed above the water around us; and another, from the stage at the Fillmore, heaving and sweaty in a burgundy T-shirt and Giants cap, curved at the brim, my parents sitting proudly in the balcony box seats, a sea of people reciting my songs along with me, admiring this room I'd been in a million times before from a new angle, now in possession of an unerasable memory, a freedom from pressure, and a belief that no matter what happened from here on out, the rest was gravy.

Humans are rarely satisfied for long. Eventually an emptiness creeps back in—a hunger for direction—and a persistent, boundless question: *Where to next?*

The White Whale would live other lives, just not with us. While we headed to the venue, Paul had a tow truck bring the bus to a transmission shop for the night, and the next morning we called our mechanic friend in Canada to handle the warranty payment.

"Warranty?" he asked, eventually acknowledging, reluctantly, he had indeed sold us the full coverage package.

"I'll fix it, no problem," he conceded. "Bring it to the shop here in Toronto anytime."

The crook also generously offered, if it was inconvenient for us to get the bus to Toronto, that we were welcome to sue him for the money from anywhere in Canada.

Fuck Canadians, I thought.

I must, however, admit that

BRAND-NEW TRANSMISSION!

was a feature I emphasized heavily when we put the bus back on Craigslist after paying yet another four thousand dollars to re-rebuild it in San Francisco.

The ethics of selling a lemon are simple: If you know it's a lemon, admit it. The tougher question is, what's a lemon? Yes, the bus was beat to shit, missing two rows of seats, had a janky door mechanism, jagged pieces of plywood where we'd knocked out the back wall, probably our residual disease colonies festering in the yellowed cushion foam, and a balky transmission. But that was a *brand-new* balky transmission, now double warranty covered across North America.

PLUS CUSTOM WOOD CUP HOLDERS!

For months we got no bites, dropping the price further and further. But finally, almost a year after we parked the bus back in the same spot in Torrance where we'd bought it, Nils and I were giving a walk-around to Rob, a Viking-size, bearded, heavily pierced and tattooed, extremely cordial bass player for a death metal band getting ready to hit the road.

We didn't tell him he was our only potential buyer, but maybe he could smell our desperation. I could definitely smell his. He'd left this important piece of planning till the last minute, just like we had, and here he was, slumming in the lowest-price bracket, where buyers don't get to be picky.

Maybe the Whale broke down a mile from the DMV, maybe it went another hundred thousand miles uphill without a twitch. I'll never know. Rob took the vehicle to a mechanic for inspection, Nils and I went to the DMV with him to sew up the paperwork, he gave us an envelope full of cash, and we shook hands. When we handed him the keys I felt that gumbo of relief and sadness that I'd seen in Eva's eyes when we first bought it.

It was a good hooptie. You can paint a piece of shit gold, but it's still a piece of shit. But sometimes a piece of shit has gold on the inside—ask Paul Hamer. A tour bus's job is not to be pretty; it's to get you there. And in the White Whale we made it, every time.

Concert Tickets

And the vomit sits there in the bathtub, the different colors in pink and orange bands, like the background of that oil painting where the man holds his cheeks and screams—*The Scream*, by whomever painted that—it looks like the sky in that painting. I know I shouldn't be dragging my finger across my own puke, cutting a trough in it, letting the trough fill in and then cutting another one, but I need to confirm that this actually came out of me, and if it did, why is it really so disgusting to touch it? To touch something with the outside of one finger, that, until a few minutes ago, was all the way inside my own stomach. Shouldn't it also be gross then that we walk around with stomachs full of vomit and guts full of shit and arms and legs full of blood all day? I guess it's gross to touch it because it came out with little bits of me clinging to it, streaks of acid and bile making the bathroom smell like tangerine and copper, because I puked until there was no more puke and all that was left to come out of me was actually myself, and if I didn't stop heaving, then I might chip away so much that if this spinning fever ever finally ends, there might not be enough left over to recognize me. Even doubled over in pain I can admire the silver claw feet of our family's most famous porcelain casket, the bathtub that's been here since the Point Reyes house was built, where they filmed *Village of the Damned*, and they actually used the bathtub in the shot, showed the claw feet and everything, and it's stupid, yeah, yeah, yeah, a movie about kids with the mental powers of humans evolved a million years in the future. Just because they're a million years smarter doesn't mean they're a million years better, but it is sad that the army kills them anyway—smart or not, they didn't deserve to die, and neither did the mice in the attic. Mom had her heart in the right place when she bought that humane, catch-and-release trap, but *humane trap* is really a contradiction in terms, plus a name like *The Mouse Hotel* just puts out weird vibes, and it must have been so much worse for them than if we'd just set regular traps and snapped their necks, but instead they had to wait there for weeks, for freedom that never came, forgotten, scratching up against the aluminum walls, piled up on top of one another, hungrier and hungrier until they finally starved, and eventually there must have been one last mouse left alive, a dozen carcasses pressing in on him, too weak to move, hoping for death to finally come, and weeks after it did, when we finally remembered about the Mouse Hotel in the attic, instead of freeing them into the garden and patting ourselves on the back for our empathy, Mom's shaking a trap full of tiny rotted ribcages into the trash—not the indoor can obviously, but the one in the garden, far away from the house, near where right before I got sick, me, Sam, and Taylor were lying on our backs looking up at the sun and the bright blue sky, when I pointed to the green pine tree in front of us and explained how it's not made of leaves but of some kind of woven fabric, corduroy I think, little strips of corduroy gliding like a conveyer belt, or those moving airport walkways, and Taylor saw it too, understood the corduroy tree in exactly the same way, and I wanted to cry because at that moment I felt more connected to her than I had ever felt to anyone, more connected than when I kissed her in my car, or on Castro Street, or when we shared a sleeping bag in Santa Cruz, and even when we're older and she fucks other people and gets married to one of them, I will always have the corduroy tree, and maybe that's what every guy who's ever watched a girl slip away tells himself, but it's good enough for me, and I resolved to be a true friend, not the kind who quietly holds out hope that things might change down the line, but a friend who can love without the expectation of anything in return—I resolved it to myself and I meant it, and then my stomach turned inside out and I ran into the bathroom. It's been only five minutes, ten maybe, staring at my puke in the bathtub when Sam and Taylor knock on the door again. *George, are you all right? You've been in there for two hours.* And who's to say which one of us is right?

◉

When you call him you have to tell him you're looking for "concert tickets." He's in my phone as "Ben the Hippy." I don't know anyone who knows his last name.

Sam and I meet Ben at the Laurel Inn on Presidio Avenue, described on a sign inside the door as A JOIE DE VIVRE BOUTIQUE HOTEL, a class of hotel I never knew existed, where he's crashing for the week.

"We're seeing our friend," we tell the concierge behind the desk, and ride up to the second floor in a gold- and mother-of-pearl–plated elevator, Muzak playing low.

We knock tentatively at the door. After a few moments it opens to a tastefully decorated suite—thick-framed hardwood mirror, glossy coffee table photography books, a king-size bed with way too many varieties and shapes of pillows, and that little strip of shimmery fabric over the bottom of the mattress that serves no discernible purpose. He hugs us like we're old friends. Ben the Hippy comes as advertised—a thick, greasy black beard and half-open eyelids, a mane of long black hair with a streak of gray starting to show at the root, barefoot, chest hair erupting from the V of his loosely-tied hotel bathrobe, looking like he broke into the hotel room from a squat up the street. Ben's girlfriend, short and plump with rosy cheeks, waves a polite but brief hello. She's dressed in socks, jeans, and the kind of worn plain gray pullover hoodie that you'd buy in bulk at Marshalls. A mixed-breed dog with a bandaged leg hobbles around the room, sniffing at strewn-about socks and underwear.

"Hey, you guys, whoa, come on in."

Ben yanks a black carry-on-size suitcase onto the Jack-and-Jill bathroom sink counter connected to the bedroom. He opens a key lock on the zipper and matrushka-dolls a smaller suitcase from the first one. After undoing a lock on the new suitcase, he pulls out a wad of newspaper and shakes a small mountain of dried gray mush-rooms, caps and stems, onto the counter—enough to pack the inside of a microwave from top to bottom.

"Space salad, man. This is gonna take you to Jupiter."

Maybe Ben the Hippy fights with his girlfriend just like everybody else. Maybe he's got liver disease, and business has been bad, and every night for twenty years he's had the same anx-iety dream where his teeth fall out. Maybe. But in my mind, Ben's the happiest guy on Earth. He has rough days but knows that every trial is a lesson. He loves his common-law wife more than he loves himself and every night he rests his head on the downy pillow of a different joie de vivre hotel, content from a day of good, honest work. Leading tours to Jupiter—the extent of his aspirations.

If that's what Ben's selling—a chance to feel that free—I'm buying.

◎

The setting sun is tangled in the antlers of a tule elk, one of a dozen grazing past the fence, and I know I shouldn't be craning my neck, since I'm the one who volunteered to drive, plus I haven't totally come down yet, but it's such a pretty picture—the charred pines, the skeletons of last summer's forest fires, a few miles from where Grandpa's buried, looking out over the ocean forever, three friends weaving through the golden hills, brittle straw glowing at the elk's hooves, antlers on fire as the sun flares out from behind his crown, dances back into its shadow, then peekaboos out again, sug-gesting if he just dipped his head to graze he'd set the hills on fire, and I squeeze the wheel in triumph because just when I think it can't get any better I remind myself that we have the greatest of all God's gifts—leftover fireworks, three beautiful twelve-inch aerial shells in the trunk—and I glide neatly into a parking space at McClures Beach with the confidence of a man who's a little bit stoned and a little in love and has shit to blow up. The path is just like it's been as long as I can remember, every stalk of tall grass a vaulting pole for a grasshopper, or a cricket, or katydid, summer-saulting childishly, showing off for the beetles and flies humming above, so dense that if you squint and unfocus your eyes it's like the field is fizzing with Pop Rocks—a flat mile of candy, that, as my stomach growls, reminds me I'm starving—strange since I had all that leftover spaghetti for lunch—strange until I remember my fin-ger cutting through the half-digested noodles in the bathtub, the exact same way me, Sam, and Taylor are cutting through the deep sandstone canyon now, snaking down the path toward the beach, between the high red cliffs, the life's work of a planet under a billion years of pressure to produce masterpiece upon masterpiece upon masterpiece, and we—three leftover fireworks—walking on top of it all. The gulley finally loogies us onto the shore, its fine tan sand spiked with boulders. Taylor skips by the big rock arches, and a lump rises in my throat like the one Mom can't hide when she talks about her high school boyfriend—emotion that forty short years can't dull, a tremor that makes me love my mother more because I understand her in those moments, relate to an ache that takes noth-ing away from our family but illuminates the million different lives each of us could have led if we'd washed up on different shores.

I grab the supplies from my little purple backpack and duct-tape the thick cardboard roll to the best base I could find at my parent's house—my Little League sportsmanship plaque from 1999—which, when I center the cardboard tube on the gold-painted plastic medallion fits perfectly—a little *too* perfectly if you ask me—and we breathe in the salty air and smile because we have a backpack full of colors and tonight the sky will be our canvas—three twentysomething nothings here to party like it's 1999, sending the universe a message of peace and love and sportsmanship.

Taylor cradles the first shell in her arms only to realize with sorrow that its wick is missing. The second mortar's wick fights valiantly against the wind, my cold, incompetent fingers slipping against the spark wheel of Taylor's crappy gas station Bic. But the green tail finally catches, showering sparks against all odds, and I drop the shell down the chute. We flee and plug our ears for a blast that never comes. Another dud.

The final wick lights easy. I plunge it down the tube and we run, the sand giving way beneath our feet, and we look up to where we expect to see the mortar rip across the sky. And then the deafening explosion comes, louder than any of us expected, a bang big enough to launch a new universe, but the heavens maintain their indifference and instead the theater comes from below, the earth erupting like a detonated landmine, sand and gravel and driftwood shrapnel radiating outward as we fling ourselves onto the beach, suddenly *inside a color*, dazzling green beams pulsing in every direction around us, caught in a glowing spider web, a three-dimensional candy-striped lightning bolt lattice, the moment throbbing and expanding—how I imagine it looks in the middle of a brain when it short-circuits, or when a person falls in love—and then the glitter fades from the sky and we lie there, sand in our shoes, ringing in our ears, the smell of gunpowder in the air.

"Holy shit!" Sam yells. We dust ourselves off and examine the launch site, the cardboard tube, banana-peeled back, dangling by a thin scrap of duct tape, my sportsmanship plaque crusted with soot. I admit that I might have/probably/definitely loaded the mortar upside down, so instead of getting barfed into outer space, it attacked the earth itself.

"My bad." I apologize for ruining everything.

But Sam and Taylor agree that it was the best possible outcome. And we pack my backpack with the garbage and my grimy Little League plaque, because we've been indoctrinated with a mantra our Northern California parents beat into us years ago: *Take only pictures, leave only footprints,* except I kind of like souvenirs and we forgot to take pictures. So if anybody asks, tell them three city kids threw an epic concert down at the beach, there was a pyrotechnic malfunction but no one was hurt too bad, and it was even better than if the show had gone according to plan because the band just laughed and played on—one encore after another, after another.

Acknowledgments

Thank you endlessly to my mom and dad; my editor, Kate Napolitano; Milena Brown, Aileen Boyle, Rebecca Strobel, Joanna Kamouh, Andrea Santoro, and everyone else at Penguin/Plume; Marc Gerald; Kevin Morrow; John Green; Adam Mansbach; Dawn McGuire; Ted and Becca at PYE; Andrew Briggs and family; Nicola; my teachers; Jackson; Brad; Nick; and the rest of my friends and family. Thanks for bringing love to my life and reminding me what's really important, every day.